# JOYCE SMITH'S RUNNING BOOK

# JOYCE SMITH'S RUNNING BOOK

**Bryan Smith**

Frederick Muller Limited
London

First published in Great Britain in 1983 by
Frederick Muller Limited, Dataday House,
Alexandra Road, Wimbledon, London SW19 7JZ.

**British Library Cataloguing in Publication Data**

Smith, Bryan *1938–*
   Joyce Smith's running book.
   1. Running
   I. Title
   796.4'26     GV1061

   ISBN 0–584–11054–5


Printed in Great Britain by
The Anchor Press Colchester Essex.

# Contents

# Acknowledgements

The author and publishers are most grateful to the following for their help in providing illustrations for this book: Peter Tempest who took the great majority of the photographs; Sankei Sports Shimbun for pictures of the Osaka marathon and Avon Cosmetics for pictures of the Avon International marathon.

# Introducing you to running

Running is one of the simplest, if not the simplest form of exercise there is. It is also the one form of exercise that virtually all of us have experienced, we can therefore identify with the athletics stars we see on television and read about in the newspaper. Most of us took part in athletics at school, in some form and know what is involved in racing. We may even know the rules and guess the effort required to take part in the international arena whether it be in a sprint or a marathon run, a jumping or a throwing event.

Perhaps it is this association through some early experience that has made athletics so popular with more and more people. Also there has never before been so much emphasis in the media on the importance of fitness and healthy living.

Running is something that can be done at all levels from the person who wants to feel just a little bit fitter to the serious athlete who aims to compete in the major competitions. Gone are the days when anyone running through the streets or in the park faced the taunts of the young boys calling "pick your knees up" or "keep it going". Today it is almost impossible to go out and avoid seeing someone in running gear. In those early days Joyce would go out as dusk fell, always in a track suit to do her training, almost dying of embarrassment at being seen. For a girl to run bare legged, except in competition, was virtually unseen. Today attitudes have changed completely. Joyce always trains in daylight apart from her second session in the winter and her training runs now arouse sentiments of admiration rather than getting her written off as an odd sort of girl.

One of the attractions of running is that it is an individual sport. You do not have to rely on anybody else or have a special area to carry out your jog, run or exercises. Footballers or hockey players need other people, their own team and opponents, to participate fully in their sport, they also need a pitch and goals just as rugby players, lacrosse players and everyone also involved in team sports do. Other individual sports, such as swimming, demand particular surroundings, but running can be done in the streets or in a local park without a special court or pitch. Even other forms of athletics can be complicated, needing a high jump area or a shot circle and so on. Running is basic, it is simple and anyone can do it without others. They can run anywhere and need minimal equipment.

There is no doubt that today athletics is a popular sport. There is plenty of television coverage of the major meetings, the press cater for the enthusiast as well as the interested layman in newspaper reports and meeting promoters are finding themselves inundated with entries from athletes. America has seen a running boom and the growth in the popularity of running can be seen all over the world. Running can no longer be regarded as just a sport, it can be part of so many aspects of your life. It does provide what has been regarded as the main area of sport and that is competition. But competition has expanded since the days when Joyce started running, today in athletics it is not only sport for all but competition for all. There are graded track meetings to cater for all abilities, there are hugely popular fun runs for those who have no wish to be involved in the more serious aspect of competition for medals or prizes. On the road many races are attracting record entries as runners test themselves out against the clock. Running also aids fitness and will

*Running and racing is an enjoyable way to keep fit. Joyce and Ingrid Kristiansen competing in a marathon in Japan.*

involve you in other factors which help your general fitness, such as exercise and diet.

Having been involved with athletics for over 20 years it is pleasing to us to see the developments now taking place in the sport. We hope we can help those who want to come into athletics and to those who are now running perhaps we can show the way to some improvement. Joyce's experiences as a club athlete, as an international athlete, and a winning female athlete from the time she did athletics at school to her present position in the veteran age group may encourage others to enjoy their running that little bit more. Ask anyone why they run and their answers will probably be along the lines of, "I enjoy it" or "I like to keep myself fit" and invariably this wish to be fit is linked to wanting to be healthy. Fitness is specific. A person may play a game of football and declare himself fit but ask him to run 10 miles and he may shudder at the thought because fitness for one sport does not mean fitness for all sports. What we are looking for basically is a general fitness that leads to a healthy existence and also enables you to lead a full and enjoyable life. After that level of fitness comes our specific fitness for running.

Consider the following diagram which was given to me at college, to me it illustrates what athletes and coaches are looking for in the search for fitness.

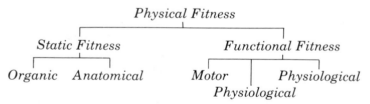

Having thrown in some special words let's explain the diagram. Physical fitness is something I hope we would all wish to enjoy but eating certain foods every day or throwing open the bedroom window on a fine morning does not necessarily make you fit—it may give you a feeling of fitness but feeling fit and looking fit can be very different to the real thing of being fit. Back to the diagram. Static fitness is something we can leave to the medical profession, that is the health factor of fitness. Organic as the name implies deals with the fitness of the body's organs, thus if we have an infection or a cough there is a problem with one of the parts of our body and we may feel unwell and to rectify it we seek the help of the doctor. Similarly with anatomical fitness, anatomy is concerned with our body structure and a broken bone is the concern of the doctor and leaves us not completely fit. However we must hasten to add that a deficit in one region of fitness does not mean an individual is relegated to the sidelines of spectating. Many people have conquered an illness or disability to enjoy sport, it may not be running but it has given them the satisfaction of achievement in the field of sport.

Functional fitness is concerned with three areas of fitness: physiological fitness which is a person's physical working capacity and includes inherited ability, muscular efficiency, the development of the heart and lungs and so on. Motor fitness results from your skill and learning of the event but will depend on such factors as flexibility, co-ordination, endurance, strength, speed and power. These factors will be discussed in more detail later but it can be appreciated now that athletes may well possess more of one factor than another. For often the difference between athletes is inherited and one athlete may possess an inborn capacity for more speed than another, or more endurance. However with training athletes can and do improve and this is what all athletes are aiming to do, improve on what they have done previously. Moving on to the third factor in functional fitness we come to psychological fitness. This part is the one that can often affect performance the greatest without athletes really appreciating it. It covers such areas as motivation, personality, social behaviour, intelligence and perception. Just think of all the questions and answers that could come under this classification. Is staleness due to boredom or a lack of motivation? Does ritual relieve stress before a race? How does one reconcile conflicting aims, adjust to the demands of running an emotional or a physical upset? Is it a good or bad thing to have a mascot? Should one wear certain

*Joyce and Lia jogging in Hyde Park.*

clothing for a race? How do disruptions in your home life affect your running? Do people consider the effects of a change of life style, or a physical change such as weight loss or a period?

Each aspect of functional fitness has only been touched upon here but in further chapters, examples and more detail will be dealt with as they become more pertinent to certain problems.

However there is one consideration with which Joyce has become particularly associated. People are always asking her about age and running. When Joyce was at school the furthest distance she could run was 150 yards and then in the 1950s and early 1960s the longest distance on the track as far as international competition was concerned was 800 metres, although one mile championships were held in most domestic championships. Cross-country races of up to three miles were held and the only road running was in road relays in which the longest run was around 2 miles. It was in 1960 that the 800 metres was re-introduced into the Olympic Games, and in 1969 the European Championships held the 1500 metres for the first time and the Olympics followed in 1972. 1974 saw the introduction of the 3000 metres on the track in the European Championships and 1982 the marathon for women comes into the European Championships. So Joyce has found an incentive to keep her going through the years and this desire to fulfil an aim is a very strong motivation factor.

At school Joyce aimed to win the school events which were 150 yards and long jump. In club athletics it turned out she could win middle-distance events 880 yards and one mile (nowadays 800 metres and 1500 metres). Being able to win at club level she aimed higher at county, then Area and eventually National. Then as new distances were introduced so came new challenges and the aims continued to be there. Now at the age of 45 Joyce is still able to maintain a place in the world ranking lists and while she continues to improve ambition remains. Veterans' athletics is growing even faster than some of the other sides of athletics. It is a huge movement in the USA. The

*The start of Joyce's career in club athletics – note grass track, the running clothes, spikes and style of track suit of the spectators.*

enjoyment of running, the feeling of being healthy and the thrill of competition is not limited therefore to one particular age group. The spectrum has opened up and running is available for all who wish to take what is offered.

While there can be no denying that eventually age can affect performance, it is attitude which has the final say in how your performance will be affected. If you say you are too old at 40 then you will be too old. If you want to feel fitter you can, if you want to improve you can, but you may have to choose your event. Age is certainly no barrier to anyone who wants to take up running as long as you have the right attitude and look for progression slowly rather than immediately. Don't forget slow progression will give you longer enjoyment.

# For the beginner

Once you have decided that athletics is going to be your sport or one of your sports, you will want to get going and start getting fit for running. Of course if you are sports-orientated you will have tried some form of running before. Running is not just for runners: football, hockey, rugby, netball, basketball, in fact many sports depend upon running in order to participate in them. If you were to think of the basics of most sports and made a list you would find that running, jumping and throwing would all be on the list and they are the components of the sport of athletics. Similarly swimming is the basic need for all aquatic sports. One of the delights of running is that it can be done anywhere but you will probably find it more enjoyable if you can run in company with others. However company is not essential and often you can have an enjoyable relaxing run just by yourself which can relieve the stresses of the working day.

The first job is to kit yourself out with the very basic needs. Acquire a pair of training shoes, socks if needed, shorts, a vest or T-shirt, and a tracksuit for cold weather is a good idea but a sweat shirt would suffice. In Britain the weather will determine what you wear as also will your fitness. A seasoned athlete in shorts and vest will generate his or her own heat on a good hard run even on the coldest winter's day but a jogger may take a mile or more to warm up and may be better off wearing a track suit. However on a sunny summer's day there is no question of trying to retain heat, the problem is to get rid of it, so shorts and vest for all. By the way it is a rule in the UK that in all competitions vests and shorts must be worn, so all you sun-tanned men remember to keep your vests on. Vests and shorts are the minimal requirements, you can wear a track suit in competitions as long as your number is pinned on the track suit and can be clearly seen.

Now you are ready and have to make a decision on how you are going to start. Is it to be a brave dash from the front door wondering who is looking from behind their net curtains or a sly creep out when it is dark hoping no one is looking out of their windows? If it is the latter remember that even though you may not want to be seen it is far safer that you should be seen. If you run at night wear something light is a saying well worth remembering.

At school pupils are introduced to athletics through the school's physical education programme and in many schools there is some competition available. It may be the school sports day with its inter-house or inter-class competitions or the school may be involved with local school leagues or competitions. Often there is a link between schools and a local athletic club, this will provide a natural progression for the athlete wanting to proceed from school to club athletics. It also helps introduce the school pupils to the wider world beyond school and thereby helps prepare pupils for their life in the adult world.

School athletics follow rules set down by the National Schools Athletics Association and similarly club athletics abide by the rules of the national associations, from whom you can obtain sets of rules. For instance in England athletes may not run in a registered marathon unless they are over 18 years old. The rules are drawn up for the protection of the athletes and to ensure that there is fair competition. There are undoubtedly many young people, still at school, wanting to run a marathon but surely athletics is not just about doing one competition; it is also about enjoyment, fitness, health, friendship and progress not for just several months or even one year but hopefully

*A young cross-country team prepared for competition.*

for many years to come. One other reason why we would advise the very young not to be determined to become marathon runners is that at a young age the athletic world is wide open to them. They may not know what event is the most suitable for them. They may have shown some potential at one event but their future potential in that or any other event is unknown. A child, could be a future world champion, but a child does not yet have the speed, endurance and strength of a champion and should not risk killing off enthusiasm for the sport at an early age. World champions in the marathon will have to run faster than 2 hours 9 minutes for men and 2 hours 25 minutes for women. That is 26 consecutive miles at just over 4 minutes 55 seconds for men and just over 5 minutes 31 seconds pace for women. Now if you cannot run one or two miles at that pace then it would be asking for the impossible to run a marathon at that pace. In fact there is a need to be able to run considerably faster over one mile in comparison to your marathon pace. You may not be aiming

11

to be a champion but you can see the stresses involved and the rules are laid down for the protection of all. So for the athletes still at school the advice is be patient, work on improving your speed if you want to make it to the top in later life. One other factor and perhaps the most important, school children have been running 800 metres, 1500 metres and cross country without any ill-effects. Marathon running can be stressful and what effects marathons may have on a growing body are unknown. This is the reason for the rules being drawn up as they are.

But back to the dreaded business of actually getting going with running. If we assume that you have left school and have no contact yet with the local athletics club, one alternative to training at home is to take a stroll down to the nearest running track which will probably be owned by the local council, and use the changing facilities there. If you do not have a local track try a leisure or sports centre, which will again generally be a local authority facility. You are looking for somewhere to change into your sports gear and after your exercise have a shower and revert back into your normal day to day clothes.

A word of warning now: the first sessions feel the worst, but once you get into running then the enjoyment of feeling better and fitter will come, as will a sense of achievement when you conquer your own yardsticks on the road to greater fitness. Indeed the first session could be spent walking more than running. Invariably when you start running you start off too fast and in a very short time have run out of breath, your legs ache and you wonder why you started. At this point take a stroll with long strides and regular breathing. Having got this far it will seem a pity to abandon all those good thoughts, the resolution that has been going through your mind for the last few months or maybe just for the last few days if you received your flash of inspiration when watching athletics on the television. When everything is normal and you can breath again without any difficulty then break into a slow jog for just one hundred yards or metres if you think metric, then walk one hundred, then jog and so the process goes on until you have done this eight to ten times and you can finish with a 150-metre run back to base whether that be your front door or the door to the dressing rooms at the local track, leisure centre or sports centre.

Then walk around to recover and get your breathing back to normal. Having started, and now completed, the first session, you can start planning and thinking about the next session. Will it be 200-metre runs and 100-metre walks or the same as last time? Was it 5 minutes or 10 minutes out last time? Can you make it 15 minutes next go? The variations are numerous but you will begin to see some progress, especially if you keep a training diary and log exactly the training you did and how you felt.

After a number of sessions you will be wondering if you should train with someone else. You may already have dragged along some unsuspecting soul from the office, or even have met someone during your first runs. Eventually you may consider joining a club, but clubs can vary quite a bit. Some provide just competitions, others try and be more of a social get together, some provide information. Shop around and find a club that will provide you with what you want. You may be lucky and find one at your local track, you may have no choice locally but once you are a member you have a voice in the organization of the club. If they

*A club training session shows the fun of friendly competition.*

don't have a jogging section can you or a friend get one going?

However we have been assuming that running is the side of athletics that interests you, distance running at that. Yet Joyce's own experience shows the danger of assuming too much too soon. Joyce started athletics at school like most people do. In those days the longest distance girls could run was 150 yards and they were also allowed to high jump and long jump. Joyce showed some aptitude for sport and could win the school 150 yards and long jump championships. She even represented the school in the Hertfordshire County Schools Championships and became County Schools Long Jump Champion. However as there was no link between school and the local club Joyce stopped athletics when she left school and that could have been the end of her athletic career, but for a holiday camp sports day which she took part in while on holiday with her parents. Competing in the camp sprints she beat a girl who had come well prepared and was dressed in a track suit covered in badges. No one would believe that Joyce wasn't a member of an athletic club so when she returned from holiday she went down to the local athletic club to join, with a view to taking up sprinting and long jumping again. There was also another reason and that was a social one. The girlfriend she was going about with had found herself a boyfriend and this was a case of two's company three's a crowd, so Joyce was then looking for more friends. At the club Joyce found that the standard was a lot higher than she expected and she was not good enough to make the club team in the sprints and long jump. Joyce found she was making up the relay team and could compete in extra races put on for those not quite good enough for the scoring events. One day she went along to a trophy meeting to support the club and on arrival was asked if she would run round, just to score points, in an 880 yards as the club had no one available. Joyce ran and surprised everyone when she broke the club record and from that day since Joyce was no longer the sprinter and long jumper hoping for competition but a middle-distance runner who could claim her own spot in the club team. It is therefore well worth trying other events to make sure you find the one that suits you best. However you may not be as fortunate as Joyce and find your event in just one tryout. It may require several attempts at different events to find the one for you.

*Sebastian Coe in full flight during an indoor race.*

You should also take into account that the more technical events will need to be persevered with longer as there is a need to learn the particular actions required.

After all, just as it takes time to learn to swim or ride a bike, it takes time to learn a high jump technique such as the Fosbury flop, or the intricacies of one of the throwing events. In some events, while the basics can be easily understood, to develop further may require the athlete to work up extra strength or mobility gradually, or any of a number of factors that could be involved in that particular event.

Athletics is an all-encompassing sport and it would be well worth looking at the various events that come under that heading. Indeed in some countries a break down has already been made and you find track and field under one label, with cross-country, road running and race walking classified as separate sports. However, in the UK we have a general classification of athletics which include the following:

> Sprints – including sprint relays
> Middle distance
> Long distance
> Cross-country
> Race walking
> Steeplechase – (men only although there have been some experimental races for women)
> Hurdles
> Shot putting
> Discus
> Javelin
> Hammer (men only)
> High jump
> Long jump
> Triple jump – (men only)
> Pole vault – (men only)
> Multi-events – decathlon for men – pentathlon and heptathlon for women

As you can see from the list above there are sixteen areas to choose from, but while our involvement is in just the distance running, don't ignore the fun and achievement of the other events.

Very often the event you are best at can be decided by your physical make up which includes your genetic

*Allan Wells shows the strength and drive of a sprinter.*

inheritance. Very often one finds that tall people go for the hurdles or high jump, sprints are those who have the ability naturally to move their legs fast, while the big people may be shot putters, discus throwers and hammer throwers. Javelin throwers have a natural ability in being

*Joyce competing in one of her early club races.*

able to throw a long way whether it be a javelin or stones. Pole vaulters have strong shoulders and a gymnastic ability while distance runners possess natural endurance. So the event you start out with or the event you first did at school may not satisfy your best potential and when joining a club it would be well worth while having a go at the different events before deciding which one you are going to concentrate on. However you do not have to tackle the one you are best suited to for the main object is to enjoy what you are doing, so go for the event you receive the most pleasure from. Learn about the event and if you can receive help from a coach so much the better.

You will certainly need a coach if you are going to do one of the more technical events (jumping or throwing) even if you require them just to act as a pair of eyes to see what you are doing and be able to pass comment on your performance. The coach can also help with planning schedules or training programmes and act as a general adviser, which includes help in preparing you for competition. Finding a coach may be a problem. The number of qualified coaches is small in comparison to the numbers who participate in the sport! Very often clubs do not have coaches for every event and a coach at the local track may have sufficient athletes under his wing and cannot take any more on. Do not despair. Very often coaches will not object to you joining in a squad training session and you will usually find other athletes will be able to advise and help you. When the time is ripe you will be able to approach a coach to seek his advice and more often than not the coach will give advice freely.

Generally however you will find yourself following a pattern as follows, especially if you are a track athlete. After your first visit to the track you will be introduced to the other athletes in the club and you will often find that you do the same sort of training as they do whatever the event. On subsequent visits you will meet up with the athletes who do the same events as you and you train together, after all athletics can be quite sociable. Then eventually you could meet up with a coach who will be able to advise you on your further progress. But you can run by yourself and many people prefer to. So don't feel you have to train with the local club. However, club membership gives you contact with the administration of your sport.

Having decided that you are going to be a competitive athlete or specialise in one particular side of the sport, now is the time to start building up on your athletic wardrobe. The pair of plimsoles you started jogging in may have been fine for that purpose but if you are going to race then you may find yourself at a distinct disadvantage in a sprint with all your rivals wearing spikes. So if you are going in for competition get the right shoes, spikes for the track or jumping events and suitable competition shoes should you be doing other events. Treat yourself to a suitable athletic vest if you are still running in your old rugby jersey or tennis shirt. After all if you are going play the part you might as well look the part.

Suitably equipped now, you may still be on your own, you may even desire to run in solitude but don't forget there are other aspects of running and fitness to take into consideration like the exercises which should prove

*A cross-country race catering for all abilities. Note how far the field of runners stretches back.*

beneficial. These are dealt with in more detail later as are different training methods.

You may not have joined a club but are looking for competition. You will find details of competitions in the athletic magazines that can be found on the shelves of the main high street newsagents. Even if you have joined a club you may still want to find your own races, instead of sticking to the club fixtures list, so keeping informed about running by purchasing one of the athletic magazines is well worth while.

Reading about your sport will often provide many answers to those questions that have been buzzing around in your head, especially in the early days. But you will soon find your knowledge growing and will be progressing to greater fitness and better performances. Don't forget champions generally only progress by points of a second. The athlete just starting out can have the satisfaction of improving by several seconds at a time.

# Fit and healthy

For those not concerned with racing, running can still provide many benefits that are generally sought after in everyday life. There are many advantages to be obtained from following a fitness course that while it may not make you into a champion, will give you the feeling of being fitter and being able to cope better with the problems of everyday life. After all, running not only tones up the muscles to enable you to do physical work better, it also seems to sharpen up the mind and give relief from the stresses modern day living can bring.

Today we are very much creatures of habit and routine. Whatever we do, generally we follow a fairly rigid routine in our daily lives. It may not be as simple as getting up, washing, breakfast, off to work, return from work, have dinner, watch television then off to bed for the end of another day. Have you ever thought about how your days pass by? It is worth while just writing down what you do. Probably you will find that your time is remarkably full. When are you going to find time to run? This is how Joyce manages her training on the days when she is not doing her part-time job. On these days she does one training run at 4 o'clock.

| | |
|---|---|
| 7.15 | get up, wash, dress, get Lia ready for school have breakfast |

| 8.45 | take youngest daughter to school |
| 9.05 | start morning training run |
| 10.00 | arrive home from training, shower |
| 10.15 | housework |
| 12.30 | lunch |
| 1.30 | make and bake cakes for the week |
| 3.00 | leave home to collect Lia from school |
| 3.30 | return home and start preparing evening meal |
| 4.30 | go out for second training session, after eldest daughter has arrived home from school |
| 5.30 | back from training run, shower |
| 6.00 | sit down for evening meal and the rest of day is usually spent doing the cleaning up, athletics club paperwork and watching television. |

As you can see a routine is easy to fall into. One of the traps is when you fall into a routine that accomplishes nothing. Find a spot in your daily or weekly routine and make it your training time. The certain way to failure is to say to yourself "I'll fit training in during one of my spare moments, I've got plenty of those". Surprisingly when it comes down to it those spare moments disappear. You've got to weed the garden, clean the car, write a letter, visit the launderette. Or you will say to yourself it is raining so I'll go out twice tomorrow. Come rain or shine if it is your training time, then train! It is surprising how enjoyable it can be running in the rain or on a crisp frosty morning. Now a word of warning, however. Having told you to go out training in all weathers and never to break the routine, beware of bad colds or if you feel you have an ailment developing. Should you be suffering from some such condition then don't train. Exposing your body to further stress could turn a cold into flu or worsen your complaint. One other time when you don't train is in the fog. Filling your lungs with fog isn't going to do you any good so don't do it. Having fitted training into your normal routine, do it regularly, but it is up to you exactly how much you are going to do. It could be twice a week, it could be once a day,

*Joyce running with an injured shoulder which brought on another injury to her knee because she was running off balance. Injuries cannot be ignored.*

often it will depend on your aims and ambitions. Running in itself is just one aspect of training and there are other areas involved with general fitness that should be considered.

If there is one area that is most often forgotten in the preparation of the distance runner it is exercises for mobility stretching and strengthening generally. It is not difficult to understand why this happens; it has often been said and rightly so that the best training for running is to run. However running only gives you a certain range of movement and in order to increase your running ability it is necessary to increase your range of movement. If we take a very simple illustration as an example: say a runner takes 50 strides in 100 metres (2 metres per stride). If greater mobility and strength can increase his or her stride length by 5 centimetres (2 inches approx) then there will be a saving of 2·5 metres (or 8 feet) which would be a stride less assuming the same leg speed is maintained. Expressed another way, it is 2·5 metres in front of a rival who previously was an equal. Remind yourself that in the 1980 Moscow Olympics Allan Wells won the gold medal by just 0·01 of a second, perhaps because he had that little bit of extra suppleness.

Exercises should be done before every training session and before every race. Not only will they help the general running movement, they also help to keep injuries away. Like many runners, Joyce has often ignored her exercises and only does them after being injured and then given exercises to do to cure the injury, when she vows to keep the exercises going. Obviously the best thing is always to do the exercises and then one hopes never to incur injury. On club training sessions we get all the distance runners to warm up together and then to go through a full routine of warm up exercises. Even when the coaches are not watching, the girls have now got into the habit of doing their exercises and it is a ritual that has been well worth establishing. However before going into an exercise routine, some very easy jogging or running should take place to get the body warmed up. There is an increase in mobility in a warm joint as opposed to a cold joint and stretching a cold joint could result in a tear or strain. Exercises can of course be done anytime and fitted into anyone's daily life. The exercises described here can be done and be beneficial for everyone, not just distance runners. A word of warning first, movement in stretching is done slowly and gently there should be no violent jerking.

## WARM-UP EXERCISES

**Arm circling**    Standing erect feet slightly apart, say about 30 cm (12 inches), circle one arm at first, inactive arm remains by the side. Active arm circles backwards brushing past the ear. Do it 6 times with the right arm, then 6 times with the left. For greater shoulder mobility try circling one arm forward while other arm circles backwards at the same time. After 20 seconds of circling arms, change over so that the arm that went forward now goes backwards.

**Side bending**    Stand with feet about shoulder width apart, head up, hands by the sides, push right hand down right side keeping body in upright position. Repeat 4 times on each side.

**Hip extension**     Take as large a stride forward as possible and keeping your back leg straight and the body upright, sink down by bending the front leg; hold in the lowest position for 5 seconds then change leg position to repeat. Repeat 4 times each side.

**Hip abduction**     Take a large stride, as in the hip extension exercise, but face the front again, keep one leg straight, body straight, and bend the other leg sink as low as possible then change leg position. Repeat 4 times.

**Hamstring stretch**     Sit on the floor, legs together and out straight in front, bend forward to touch toes. Try for a count of 3, then relax, then repeat aiming to reach further.

Repeat 5 times. If you can touch your toes try holding your toes, knees bent, then slowly walk out on heels until legs are straight, or alternatively how far can you reach past your toes?

**Hamstring stretch**    In sitting position hold your instep, right hand to right instep or vice-versa and try to straighten leg.

**Trunk turning**    Sit on the floor, hands behind your head, turn and try to touch your left knee with your right elbow—keeping both legs apart, straight and flat on the floor. Come upright and change for left elbow to touch right knee. Alternate 10 times.

**Spine extension**    Lie face downwards on the floor, hands under the shoulders, palms flat down. Keeping hips on the floor, head back, push upwards by straightening your arms as far as possible. Hold for 5 seconds, then repeat 3 times in total.

**Calf and Achilles stretch**    Stand about 3 feet (1 metre) from a wall, both hands on the wall for support, keeping both feet flat on the ground. Now bend your elbows. You will feel a stretching on the muscles and tendon at the back of the leg. Hold for 5 seconds, then relax. Repeat 5 times.

**Abductor and adductor stretch**      Stand facing bar or hurdle about 3 feet high, an arm's length away, both hands on the bar, weight on the ball of one foot. Swing the non-weight-bearing leg left then right 20 times, gradually aiming to swing the leg until the heel rises above the level of the bar. Change legs and repeat with other leg.

**Quadriceps stretch** (1) Sit on heels, toes pointed, knees on the ground. Lean back as far as possible to produce a stretching along the top of the thighs, hold for 10 seconds. Use your hands to support you behind at first but if you can manage without, so much the better.

(2) Stand on one leg, hold foot behind you, left hand holding left foot or right hand to right foot. Gently pull foot up until you feel a stretching in the thigh. Hold for a few seconds then change legs. Use free hand for balance by holding bar or resting free hand against a wall.

31

## STRENGTHENING EXERCISES

**Press ups or Push ups**    Lie face downwards on the ground palms on the ground, hands under the shoulders, body to be kept perfectly straight as you use your arms to push to straight position. Repeat to your own personal target.

If you are unable to achieve press ups from the above position, start with your feet on some stairs, say 5 steps up, then continue until you can do 10 press ups. Next time rest your feet on the fourth step. Eventually by daily progression you will be able to do press ups from the usual position.

# ABDOMINAL EXERCISES

These exercises are progressively harder. Work your way up from number 1 to number 3.

(1) Lie on your back with legs together, hands on the thighs. Slide hands forward to touch knees, then return to original position. Your feet must stay on ground all the time. Repeat as often as the exercise is comfortable.

(2) Lie on your back with hands behind the head and elbows forward. Sit up and at the same time raise one knee so that the right elbow meets the left knee then vice-versa. Repeat as much as you can without strain.

(3) Lie on your back, hands behind your head, keeping legs straight and feet on the ground, without being held, sit up then sink back slowly. Again repeat while it is comfortable to do so.

NOTE: It is worth doing the spine extension exercise, previously described, after doing abdominal exercises.

Exercising the body may be described as the output of the engine, the input is the food we eat. If you are keen to make sure you get the most out of your body and train hard, be careful about what you put in. Like a car, you put petrol in to make it go and if you drive slowly a tank of petrol will go a long way, should you drive fast then the petrol will be used up quickly. The human body will use up more fuel if it is working hard than it would sitting in a chair. However, unlike the car, if the human body hasn't used up all the fuel it doesn't have a fuel gauge and surplus intake becomes fat. Fortunately this fat can still be used as a fuel but the process is slow and if the fat is not used up it becomes all too obvious. There are three basic categories of food: proteins provide building elements for the body, they help growth and repair of body tissues; carbohydrates provide energy and are the foods that do so most readily and thirdly fats which can also provide energy but not so quickly as carbohydrates do. Failure to use up both carbohydrates and fats as energy will result in body fat. Two other important elements of our diet are minerals and vitamins which both help regulate the body's processes. For instance iron, a mineral, helps in the transportation of oxygen around the body and without oxygen the body cannot burn the fuels to produce energy. Self-designed diets can be dangerous because people tend to ignore the importance of minerals and vitamins. A lack of these elements in a diet can lead to illness so if you have to diet or feel you should go on a diet it would be wise to consult your doctor or a dietician.

Many people think that just by taking exercise they will lose weight quickly and exercise is the solution to their weight problem. Exercise does require more fuel and if you do not eat any extra you will lose weight, but very slowly. People who take up running often find that they do not lose weight but put it on. This could be due to two reasons: one, they start eating more and they are not exercising enough to use up the extra fuel they are taking in and secondly they are building up muscle tissue which is heavier than fat tissue. While they might be losing fat the muscle replacement is causing a weight increase. Eventually of course there will come a time when the muscles have toned up sufficiently in response to the exercise and then weight will start to drop. It is well worth investing in a good pair of bathroom scales as a regular check on your weight will tell you when to cut down on food or increase exercise. It is necessary to find the right balance so that you maintain the weight which is best for you. It is impossible in general terms to say how much a person of such a build or height should weigh. Some people have different bone construction or muscle type and this is inherited. There are three basic body types: mesomorph – the muscle type, endomorph – the tubby type and the ectomorph or thin type. Rarely will a person fit exactly one of these categories but have some attributes of each.

We have often heard young girls state they did not want to do any exercise because they did not want to become muscular. If they are inclined to be muscular they will become so whatever because they are genetically endowed with more defined muscles. The answer to those who are worried about the effects of exercise is to look at photographs of champions and note that they do not all fall into one special body type.

What is common in most distance runners is that they do not carry too much excess weight. The effect of carrying extra weight can easily be assessed. You have noticed the difference between walking to the shops with empty shopping bags and the return journey with full bags. Imagine what it would be like to run with a car tyre around your middle, it would certainly slow you down. Extra body weight does exactly the same thing.

Joyce always keeps a check on her weight by weighing herself at the same time of the day on the bathroom scales. This is important as obviously your body weight will vary at different times of the day, perhaps the best time is first thing in the morning after getting up. It is worth recording the weight exactly in your diary so that you can look back to your good runs and note your body weight at that time, thereby finding your optimal weight. While Joyce does not usually follow any diet there have been occasions when she has gone on a special diet to get rid of a couple of extra pounds. Joyce will follow this diet for a couple of days until her weight comes down to her racing weight but for no longer than one week.

No butter or margarine, alcohol or salad oil.
Eat only lean meat.
Drink black coffee/tea (Joyce takes lemon tea with no sugar).
Breakfast every day – grapefruit, 1 or 2 eggs, coffee

| MONDAY | lunch | fresh fruit salad as much as you like |
| | dinner | 2 eggs, salad, 1 slice of dry toast, grapefruit, coffee |
| TUESDAY | lunch | cold chicken, tomato, grapefruit |
| | dinner | steak, tomato, lettuce, cucumber, celery, coffee |
| WEDNESDAY | lunch | Eggs, tomatoes, coffee |
| | dinner | 1 lamb chop, celery, cucumber, tomato, coffee |

THURSDAY    lunch   as for Monday
            dinner  2 eggs, cottage cheese, 1 slice
                    of dry toast, boiled cabbage
FRIDAY      lunch   2 eggs, spinach, coffee
            dinner  fish, salad, 1 slice of dry
                    toast, grapefruit, coffee
SATURDAY    lunch   2 eggs, spinach, coffee
            dinner  steak, celery, cucumber, tomato,
                    coffee
SUNDAY      lunch   as for Monday
            dinner  chicken, tomatoes, carrots,
                    cabbage, grapefruit, coffee

Where amounts are not specified any amount may be eaten, water can be taken with meals at any time. Again this diet is not to be followed for more than a week and usually Joyce can come off it after a few days as she is then back to racing weight. The diet is usually only needed if Joyce has had a lay off due to injury and couldn't train, or has been having an easy spell. It may only be necessary once in 18 months. When dieting never do anything to extremes. People who want to slim often leave out all carbohydrates, but because 1 gram of glycogen (a by-product of carbohydrate) stores 3 grams of water, the effect is to lose water rather than fat. Carbohydrate is also needed for good muscle and nerve metabolism.

Our day to day diet does not follow any particular pattern but we try to eat foods that will be of benefit to us, such as wholemeal bread to increase our fibre intake, and we also eat fresh fruit every day. Like most housewives Joyce tries to vary the daily family dinner but liver is usually on the menu once a fortnight because of its excellent iron content. Joyce, like most top athletes, supplements her diet with iron tablets, as iron assists in the distribution of oxygen around the body. She also takes vitamin C which helps maintain a healthy body and vitamin B (brewers' yeast tablets) which aids energy release within the body. But most people will find their ordinary diet perfectly adequate for their sporting needs. Joyce has experienced anaemia at different times in her career and so has a need to maintain the iron content in her body. Women need to watch this more than men because of their monthly loss of blood. One of the signs of anaemia is a general feeling of tiredness and your running standard falls off considerably. Your doctor can give you a blood test to diagnose if there is a drop in iron content if you suspect something like anaemia.

However, your doctor won't be too happy if you keep calling on him once a week or so to inquire about an aching limb, blisters or the minor complaints that seem to bug runners. For many of these problems a knowledge of first aid can help you out. Pulled muscles, strains and sprains do hit runners, generally when they are least expected. But a foot in a pothole or running across uneven ground, even a sudden change of direction or change in speed can result in a pain shooting up from the injured joint or muscle. If this happens to you, get home as soon as you can, take the weight off the injured limb and place some ice, wrapped in cloth, around the affected area. This will increase the blood circulation in that area and help reduce swelling thereby keeping the joint or limb moving.

The next day the joint or muscle may still be stiff. Then it needs to be slowly stretched and warmed up before any exercise is taken. If you have a sprained ankle you may find the joint is not strong enough to bear too much weight or be free enough to run on. Then exercising the foot by making as big a circle as possible with the toes and moving the foot up and down from the ankle joint will help the rehabilitation. The exercises will be replacing your running time. If the pain persists then you may need to take a trip to the casualty department of the local hospital for an X-ray.

Sometimes after a twisted ankle or a bump into a hard object bruising takes place which may be followed by some stiffness. This will not help your running so you must try and bring the bruise out. This can often be done by the 'hot and cold' treatment. Two bowls of water are required, one as hot as your hand can stand without burning and one cold, with some cubes of ice to keep it cold. Put a flannel in each bowl and alternate the flannels on the affected part, not keeping them on too long or the area becomes too used to the heat or coldness of the flannels. Each flannel should be applied 6 or 8 times and the injury should be treated twice a day, or perhaps more often if there is a lot of stiffness. A similar type of treatment can be given if you suffer from stiff or painful feet. After making sure the hot bowl is not too hot put a foot in the hot bowl and just as soon as it has become accustomed to the heat put it into the cold water. So instead of placing flannels onto the bruise you are putting the whole foot into the bowls.

One of the parts of the body that causes many runners suffering is the Achilles tendon. This is the narrow protrusion at the back of the ankle.

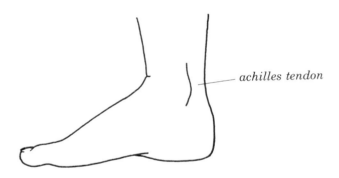

achilles tendon

This tendon connects the calf muscle to the heelbone and with the constant contraction and relaxation of the calf muscle in the running movement the Achilles tendon is for ever being stretched and relaxed. If it is not used to this or is suddenly put under more strain it reacts and becomes painful and swelling is seen around the tendon. Ice will help if you put it on the side of the tendon immediately the pain or swelling is noticed and the next day and every day from then on carry out the stretching exercises mentioned earlier in this chapter. Also during every spare moment do foot circling and up and down movements of the foot from the ankle. Training must be reduced or stopped for the next few days and recommenced when the swelling goes down. Do not massage the tendon yourself as you could be simulating the action that caused the problem. One aid that we have found does help the problem is the insertion into the heels of your shoes of sorbothane heel pads. These help absorb the impact of the heel strike on the ground and thereby reduce the shock wave that goes up the body. You can buy the pads at good sports equipment shops.

Moving up the leg to the knee joint one of the problems Joyce has suffered from is runner's knee or chondromalacia. This gives a pain around the knee cap (patella) and Joyce has got rid of this by going through a series of exercises which involve the contraction or tightening of the quadriceps, the top muscles of the thigh. The muscles are tightened for 3 or 4 seconds and then relaxed, then tightened and relaxed for 25 or 30 times and this would be repeated every few hours.

Items such as cuts, grazes etc. should be cleaned up as in normal first aid practice. A bad graze may cause a tightening of the skin so training may have to be adapted by some easy jogging until you can gain reasonable mobility. Blisters fall into two categories: those that you can run with without too much discomfort, which can be covered up with a plaster (the smooth surfaced type is best as they reduce rubbing) and the second type of blister are those that you can feel as you walk or run. These need to be broken with a sterile needle, bathed with surgical spirit and dressed to reduce any rubbing of the skin.

One hopes never to experience injuries or similar problems and if you can avoid them by taking adequate precautions so much the better. Prevention is better than cure. Following the stretching exercises suggested, making sure you have well fitting shoes, adequate warming up all help to prevent injuries. Some injuries over the years may be unavoidable unless you wrap yourself up in cotton wool. But do not always think the pain or problem will go away, Seek advice whether it be from your doctor, a physiotherapist or people who you run with. Often another athlete has had the complaint you are suffering from and will be able to recommend a sports injury practitioner who cured him or her.

Cases of stress fractures of bones which at first seem to

be a problem in adjoining muscles are the type which can only be diagnosed by a doctor after X-rays have been taken. A stress fracture is a small break in a bone, sometimes known as a hair-line fracture as it produces a very thin break. These fractures are caused by a stress on the bone often by muscle or tendon tension. The cure is complete rest until the bone has healed. Joyce has suffered stress fractures several times in her career. A stress fracture of the fibula (the smaller of the two lower leg bones) was eventually discovered after Joyce had been running badly for a couple of months. Another fracture was in the foot and the pain with that was such that she couldn't walk properly let alone run, yet although it happened during a race, Joyce didn't notice it until after she crossed the finish line. At the time Joyce thought she had an attack of cramp. The latest stress fracture was in the pelvis and the pain was in the abdomen when she attempted to run. In all these cases it was only by X-ray that the fracture was discovered. However, stress fractures are rare complaints for the average runner.

Another injury caused by tension of muscle tendons on the bone is shin soreness or shin splints which is a pain along the shin bone (tibia). This is sometimes caused by running on different types of surface. Middle-distance runners sometimes experience this when they start training on a hard track after running on grass as sometimes happens in the transition from the cross-country season to the track season. Joyce had shin soreness while training only on the road and the cause was a dropped arch which was putting a strain on the inside of the leg. After diagnosis an arch support provided the cure. Orthotic insoles have been provided to cure many a foot, leg or back problem but only after consultation with the medical profession. In fact in all cases of injury, when in any doubt see your doctor.

Your dentist should also see you regularly. One athlete we knew, a very good one in fact, found his performances deteriorating for no apparent reason until a visit to his dentist revealed some bad teeth, as soon as they were put right his race times picked up considerably!

This chapter can be quickly summarized: if runners follow a routine, exercise regularly, eat sensibly and keep clear of injuries then they will remain healthy and fit and able to enjoy their running.

# Kitting out

Joyce has an athletic wardrobe which contains a variety of running vests, a number of track suits and different types of running shoes amongst her running gear. All have been collected together over the years and serve her on different occasions depending on the events, the conditions and the mood they are required for. We would not dare suggest that you have to pay your bank manager a visit in order to fully equip yourself for running. What we do suggest is that you should build up your own athletic wardrobe slowly so that eventually you have something for all conditions. The items referred to in this chapter are mentioned so that you will have some idea of what might be necessary in the future. But the very basics will serve you well in the first place, what you buy after that adds to the luxury of choice.

The variety of clothing and shoes available to the runner is tremendous and it can be obtained not just from sports shops but also from a range of high street stores and by mail order. Look in the athletics journals for advertisements to tell you about suppliers if you don't know where to go.

Everything you buy to run in must be comfortable and nothing more so than the shoes you wear. After all they have got to see you through hundreds of thousands of footsteps. There is no substitute for trying shoes on, it doesn't matter what colour the shoes are, what they are made of or how they are designed. Unless they are comfortable to you when you are running in them they are not the shoes for you.

Joyce learnt this lesson the hard way. On a trip abroad Joyce purchased a particular brand of shoe which was popular in those days and started to wear them but couldn't break them in so that they were comfortable. Thinking that it must only just be a question of time before they would fit well, she persevered with these shoes only in the end to be put out of action with inflamed Achilles tendons. Joyce gave up wearing the shoes but the damage had been done and it took several months of physiotherapy and eventually two injections to put right. It also resulted in Joyce not being able to do very much sprinting or speed running in her training as this brought back the inflammation of the tendon. Now Joyce always makes sure that the backs of her running shoes are not high (see diagram) and if they are we cut them down to make sure they do not aggravate the Achilles tendon.

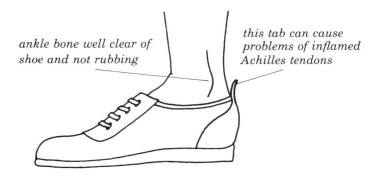

*ankle bone well clear of shoe and not rubbing*

*this tab can cause problems of inflamed Achilles tendons*

You must also be careful that the shoes do not rub on the ankle bone as this can cause soreness. Some people do have a low ankle bone and they should make sure they purchase a low-cut shoe. Generally shoes should be very comfortable to wear, have sufficient room in them to wiggle your toes and if you can have a try out run in them so much the better. If they are uncomfortable from the start don't think they will improve, or become more comfortable, should that ever happen you could well be down with an injury by then. Having found a pair of comfortable fitting shoes what other factors should you be looking for in the shoes? After all you may be faced with a choice of styles in the same make of shoe or even a choice between makes and styles.

Generally the first consideration is what exactly you are going to use the shoes for. If it is a jogging shoe you need a sole and heel that will absorb the pounding around the roads and today you can buy shoes that have an absorbing layer of rubber incorporated into the sole which makes running that much more comfortable. Should you be looking for a racing shoe then you may want to consider a lighter shoe so that you do not have to worry about carrying too much extra weight. However here you will have to take into account the benefits of a lighter shoe against the protection of a heavier but more shock-absorbing shoe.

Joyce is fortunate in that her shoes are supplied by the manufacturer but she will always go to a race with several pairs of shoes in her bag. One pair of shoes will serve her to warm up in, those are usually the general training/jogging shoes. Then she will change into a racing shoe just before the start of the race. Often the type of road surface is the deciding factor here. If the road is good tarmacadam then a very light pair can be used, if it is a gritty road then a slightly heavier pair with a thicker sole would be needed so that the stones and grit cannot be felt as you run over them.

Some people will vary their shoes also according to the distance to be run. For a 10-kilometre or 6-mile race they might wear a light pair as they will only be racing for between 30 and 50 minutes, whereas for a marathon they would wear a heavier pair as they are on their feet for very much longer and their legs have got to take much more of a pounding. What is best for you will become apparent with experience but in general once you have found a make and style of shoe that suits you it is best to stay with it as shoes do vary between makes. Some are wider than others, some have a different heel cut. Even different styles of lacing can affect the comfort.

Don't forget that shoes must be suitably 'broken in' or worn in before you race in them or even before you attempt a long run. Wear them around the house when they are new, then walk out in them, a jog of 2 or 3 miles follows, then several 5-mile runs. Gradually build up to a 10-mile training run. If there have been no problems your shoes are ready to race in.

So far we have been discussing training and road racing shoes. It is also necessary to consider track shoes and spikes. Like all other shoes, spiked shoes must fit comfortably and should feel part of the foot when you are wearing them. Fortunately spikes today are made so that you can change the actual spike on the sole according to the type of surface you are going to run on.

When going to a competition be prepared for all eventualities. At the time of the 1972 Olympics in Munich the firm that made the shoes Joyce wore brought out a new track racing shoe suitable only for all-weather tracks. This shoe did not have spikes but plastic wedges and was, of course, quite different to the standard running spike. The shoes were passed by the governing body of the sport and Joyce did race in the Olympics in them but not before several training sessions on the track in them. In 1974 Joyce was competing in the 3000 metres in the European Championships and this event was on the first day of the Championships. As is customary at championships the athletes were called for the event and numbers and spikes were checked. Joyce and another athlete presented for inspection the track shoe with these plastic wedges and the official doing the inspection rejected them. The other athlete was then at panic stations. It was 10 or 15 minutes before start time and she had no replacement. Joyce always carries a spare pair of standard spikes so just reverted to those shoes. So do be prepared.

Today track athletes need to carry a variety of different spikes to go into their shoes so they can leave the decision right up to the last minute to change spikes. Likewise spare laces should be carried – so often laces have snapped

*Spikes for different conditions. The first two spikes are for use on indoor tracks or synthetic surfaces, the middle two are for synthetic tracks only and the last two are for use on cinder tracks or cross-country.*

when runners give them an extra, but often unnecessary tug. It can be said that a spare pair of shoes is not really necessary but we have seen athletes' shoes ripped in a heat by another runner accidentally scraping over a shoe in a race. The athlete with the torn shoe needed another pair for the final. Obviously this is an extreme case but it is worth keeping in mind when buying a new pair of shoes not to just throw away the old pair. Track shoes like road shoes do vary in sole and heel design. Some have a slightly built up heel and if you are a long distance track runner you may find these to your liking.

Even with built-up heels and cushioned inner-soles athletes still have problems and Joyce has in recent years found a special rubber heel pad most useful to absorb the pounding of the roads. So often you can adapt the shoes you are most accustomed to with an insert which is very much cheaper than trying to find another style of shoe to fit you and rectify a problem.

Before leaving the subject of shoes, remember if you run with socks on then have a similar type of sock with you when you try on a new pair of shoes. I have heard of people who have tried on a pair of shoes in a woollen pair of socks but race in cotton socks. There is a vast difference in the thickness between different materials so be aware of the problem.

Coming on to socks it is up to you to decide if you want to wear them or not. Many people do not but if you do then think of comfort. Socks if worn, must be comfortable and well fitting. Not tight yet not loose, they should not crease under the foot and in general if you wear socks you should not be aware of them. Socks should be of a material that absorbs moisture and needless to say should always be clean. Ladies may like to try wearing tights in the cold weather, it is something Joyce has tried and has found to increase the comfort of running. The men will find that olive oil rubbed on their legs will provide adequate cold weather protection for them.

Shorts come in various designs and you will have to try out different styles until you find one that suits you. Shorts should give you freedom of movement, so make sure you can lift your knees high without the front of the shorts cutting into the top of your thighs. It is also worth checking that the material the shorts are made of does not become transparent when wet. Don't forget you run in the rain and sunshine.

Running vests vary a great deal and you will need to have a variety to wear according to conditions. In one of the Tokyo marathons Joyce changed from a T-shirt style running top to a sleeved top just minutes before the start and in the 1982 London marathon it was a last-minute decision whether Joyce was going to wear a T-shirt under her marathon vest or not. In the end it was decided not to as the weather forecast was for a warm start to the day. There is therefore a need to have a variety of vest styles in your running gear cupboard. T-shirts are an old favourite and can be used for training and racing. The sleeveless running vests are popular and often seen on the running track. When you join a club it is worth purchasing a club vest which is usually this style as this gives you an identification and in championships it is often a rule that club vests must be worn. It is surprising how helpful it is to spectators and fellow team members if you wear a club vest. You can often pick a person out in a large field of runners by identifying the vest.

A long-sleeved top should also be included in your running wardrobe and can be used for both training and racing in during the winter months. You need to keep warm as a warm body is more efficient, but again some people find they warm up very quickly and don't feel the cold whereas there are others who notice the cold and are worried by it.

*Joyce and Jill Clark competing in the 1981 National Cross Country Championships, both wearing club vests and shorts, but Joyce who notices the cold has additional clothing.*

British summers can be hot and humid and a marathon vest can keep the body cool. It may seem odd that in the winter you are keeping the heat in but in the summer you want to get rid of the heat. Remember that the human being is a warm blooded animal and operates at 37°C or 96.8°F. If you can keep close to that temperature by adjusting the clothing you wear, so much the better. We have found that the marathon vest with its string mesh to allow air to reach the body is better slightly loose, or certainly not skin tight. A looser vest allows air to circulate around the body better. However, do not be tempted into wearing a vest that is too large as you will always be hoisting the shoulders up or find it flapping around you. Remember comfort comes first.

I remember one unfortunate occasion when a tighter vest would have been beneficial. There was one national track final which Joyce was competing in and the competition was good with several internationals from other countries taking part. The runners were bunched as they gathered for the final sprint during the final lap and Joyce's vest was pulled when she was making her effort. Obviously if this had been spotted by the judges the culprit would have been penalized but had Joyce had a tighter man-made fibre material vest there would have been no spare vest to grab hold of. In short track races there is no concern about cooling the body down so it does not matter so much about the style of vest.

The next essential is a track suit or warm clothing for when you are preparing to race or train and also to put on after exercise. Most track suits now are made with nylon or similar fibre-based material and can be put in the washing machine. It is worth checking the label because your track suit will take a battering and can be soaked in the rain, be mud splattered and will also soak up perspiration so it could be in the washing machine quite often. A full-length zip in the jacket is common now and makes it easy to take on or off. Trousers vary from tapered legs to flared bottoms, again personal choice will be the deciding factor. If you train in track suit trousers frequently you may decide you like something that will not flap around you ankles and select a tapered leg trouser. If you prefer to train in shorts and just want something to wear to and from the dressing room then you might like a flared track suit trouser which can often double up as a leisure suit to potter around the home in.

*Track suits help keep you warm when training on cold winter days.*

For those who do not think they will want or use a full track suit very much a popular substitute for the track suit jacket is the sweat top, a long-sleeved pullover top usually made of heavy cotton and fleecy lined to keep the wearer warm. Many clubs have their logo printed on sweat tops to sell to their members. Some have a hood as part of the sweat top and as one of the areas from which there is great heat loss is the top of the head, these are useful in the winter to retain warmth in the body.

Some people wear a woollen hat to keep the head warm but this must depend on whether you find this comfortable.

*A hooded top stops heat loss through the head.*

Having tried running both with and without a hat, you certainly do feel warmer on those cold winter days with something on your head. Joyce has also often raced and trained in the winter with a ski band over the head and ears. This helps keep the hair in place and the ears warm. If you are keeping your head warm then you may feel the cold more than other people. It is therefore worth considering wearing gloves or mittens. Again it is surprising if you keep your hands warm it seems to give you a general feeling of warmth. You may have seen pictures of runners in sleeveless vests with gloves on.

Having obtained shoes, shorts, running vest, track suit, or sweat top, gloves and woollen hat what should you wear when you want to train on a typical winter evening in the rain? The best thing is to leave off the track suit because wet track suits take time to dry out whereas shorts and vests can easily be washed and dried. The alternative is to wear a wet suit or rain suit – a nylon over-suit coated on the inside and shower proof. This enables you to train without getting too wet, the one problem is that while they keep rain out they keep perspiration in so you can still come home with damp kit. The alternative to the wet suit is a Gortex suit which is made from a special treated material which keeps the rain out and also allows the perspiration to leave the suit. For the Gortex suit to work efficiently it is necessary to wear thermal underwear

*When running at night wear something white.*

which does not absorb perspiration but transports it away from the skin.

An athlete's bag often contains a variety of kit, as you may have guessed already, but it also should contain other useful items: safety pins for your race numbers, Vaseline to put around toes and other parts that may rub, olive oil for legs should it be cold, toilet paper in case the track loo has run out. If you are a track runner include a variety of screw-in spikes and spike spanners. It is advisable to Vaseline or grease the screw-in spikes to stop them rusting into the shoe.

# Planning ahead

Training must have some purpose, which is not necessarily racing. You can train to keep fit, to lose weight, to recover from an injury, to improve or to socialize with friends. Whatever you train for, know why you are doing it and if you are going to compete you should also have an aim. It may be for the next race or it may be for a championship later in the season. If it is the latter you will use smaller races as stepping stones to the major race.

The need to plan and prepare for races is very important and it applies just as much if you are aiming to win the race or are running to achieve a personal best. Training is therefore geared towards a major race not every race, indeed some races would be regarded as part of training. Several times during recent years Joyce would have raced for her club but usually only after training in the morning and using the afternoon club race as a second session.

Let me illustrate the point of using races as trials and for preparations. In the summer of 1974 Joyce was training specifically for the 3000 metres in the European track and field Championships. In the National Championships Joyce went from the gun in her heat for a fast time and ran a British record which was at the time the second fastest time in the world. In the final the next day she was content to stay with the pack to try out her finishing sprint which was used to good effect and gained a 10 seconds lead on the final lap. The races were used firstly as a confidence booster to show Joyce she could run as fast as most of the top runners in the world and also that she could put in a fast finish if need be. As it turned out Joyce came back from the European Championships with a bronze medal.

Earlier in 1972 Joyce went to the Olympics in Munich for the 1500 metres, an event in which fast times were expected. Joyce has very little basic speed so her training had to be geared to being able to run at a fast pace, for her, but for a longer distance. We were looking for speed endurance. This would give Joyce, we hoped, the ability to hang on to a fast pace during the 1500-metres race. In her semi-final Joyce ran a British record of 4 minutes 9·4 seconds during which she was timed at 2 minutes 8 seconds for the last 800 metres. This was faster than any 800-metres race Joyce had ever run (her best is 2 minutes 8·8 seconds) and reassured us that training had been on the right lines.

Also in 1972, Joyce was selected to run 1500 metres for Great Britain against the German Democratic Republic and the Netherlands. We had noted that the East Germans had a habit of going off very fast in their races and so Joyce ran sessions of repetition 300 metres and 400 metres starting fast and having a very short recovery time to get used to the type of race that could be expected. It is therefore useful to know who you are competing against and this could be someone in your club or town who you wish to beat just as well as rivals in international competitions. We will read athletic magazines and watch athletics on television to note how possible rivals run, in order to try and work out ways to beat them. Should you be competing over road or country in addition to knowing your rivals it is very useful to know the course.

However details such as knowing how your rivals run or the type of course you will be running over in your main marathon of the year have to be fitted into a full training programme that will prepare you for the competition or competitions you wish to do specially well in. No matter what the event, whether it be the Olympic Games or the local town 6 miles it is necessary to train and prepare for it.

If the competition is next week then it will be difficult to prepare a plan of training, but assuming you are planning well ahead then you can be fully prepared for the race or races you have marked in your diary as number one. If we look first of all at the typical British year there are several main competitions the athlete can aim for. Generally the athletic year has the following pattern:

## WINTER

| | |
|---|---|
| *October/February* | Road relays and cross-country league matches |
| *December/January* | County cross-country championships |
| *January* | Inter-county cross-country championships |
| *February* | Area cross-country championships |
| *February* | National indoor championships |
| *February/March* | National cross-country championships |
| *March* | International indoor competition |
| *March* | International cross-country championships |

Incorporated into this will be such events as school championships, district championships and club championships. According to your ability there will be one particular race important to you.

## SUMMER

Throughout the summer, fixture lists will contain league matches, trophy events and various open meetings but again there will be the major events one or two of which will be important to you. In Britain the events usually have the following patterns:

| | |
|---|---|
| *May* | County championships |
| *May* | Inter-county championships |
| *June* | Area championships |
| *July* | National championships |
| *August* | International fixtures |
| *September* | Major international championships. |

Obviously, in other countries the seasonal breakdown will be different from the British one.

Each fixture follows a progression so that you can aim to gradually climb the ladder to the top. For example at school an athlete first gains selection to represent the school, perhaps by doing well in the school sports. Then pupils compete for the school in the district sports, then the County Schools Championships and if good enough they would represent the county at the National Schools Championships. Then the very best school athletes go on to represent their country in international schools competitions. Then when one leaves school there is a similar ladder to climb in the club situation.

Having decided which competitions you are going to do or want to take part in you can now start planning your training. It may well be that you will also compete in the winter so you have two periods of competition. Having got as far as deciding what competition you want to enter you must consider other factors. What about holidays? What about the change over from summer track to winter cross country? What commitments do you have to your club or school? Having taken these into consideration you could well end up with a plan like this:

| Feb/Mar | Apr/May | June/Jul/ Aug | Sept | Oct/Nov/ Dec/Jan |
|---|---|---|---|---|
| winter competition period | preparing for summer competition | summer competition period | rest or change over period | build up period and preparing for winter competition |

Each period must be considered as building upon what has been done before and as a foundation for the future so that progress can be maintained not just in the few months of a competition period but year after year.

However, the novice runner may have different preoccupations. In the first instance the requirement is to get yourself fit for running and then for racing if that is what you want to do. Initially the new runner could follow the first 5 weeks' training of the beginner's marathon schedule which is set out in Chapter 8. Then in the sixth week start to concentrate on the branch of athletics which seems most attractive.

Preparing for a marathon would be slightly different to the plan above. Marathons are not the type of race which you can satisfactorily run every week or even every month. So, often a training plan should ideally be made to suit the individual, taking into account each athlete's strengths and weaknesses. How often can he or she run well over a marathon course in a year? How long a recovery period does the individual need? How long a preparation period is required? What is the level of competition?

Someone setting out to run their first marathon could easily make a plan out which has 51 weeks of race preparations with one-week competition period and that week would be the week of the marathon. Runners who run three or four marathons a year might well break the year down as follows:

| Feb/Mar/ Apr | May | June/July/ Aug | Sept | Oct/Nov/ Dec | Jan |
|---|---|---|---|---|---|
| competition preparations | race and recovery | competition preparations | race and recovery | competition preparations | race and recovery |

If you are to race well you must train well but to train well good planning is needed. Planning is an area that must not be forgotten, and applies not just to the distance of the race but also who your rivals might be. Become a strategist. With each race you learn a little bit more about the race, your rivals and also yourself. In each of Joyce's marathons she has discovered different lessons that hopefully enable her to progress to better performances. After each marathon the performance is analysed and future training adapted to benefit from the lessons learned. To illustrate this here is an account of Joyce's marathon races.

Joyce's first marathon was only 5 years ago: the 17th June, 1979, the Women's National Championships at Sandbach, Cheshire. The race drew quite a bit of publicity as it was the first marathon for several of the competitors.

*Inspection of a marathon course in Osaka.*

Probably because it was the first for several of the women, caution was the operative word and while a bunch ran together very steadily through the first 10 miles, up front one female competitor had a 3-minute lead on Joyce and the rest of the group of female runners.

*The same spot during the race. The runners were prepared for the sharp angle after the bridge.*

Panic set in at the 10-mile station when Joyce learnt of the situation and she and her club mate Carol Gould, set off in fast pursuit of the leader. They succeeded in catching the leader but in doing so had run too fast in the middle part of the race. Fortunately that burst in the middle part of the race eventually took Joyce right away from the rest of her competitors and although she suffered in the final two miles her lead was long enough to see her safely home in 2 hours, 41 minutes and 36 seconds for a new British record. It was essential that Joyce learnt some pace judgement.

Race number two was on 22nd September, 1979 in Waldneil, West Germany in the Avon Cosmetics International Race with competitors from all over the world. This race is a women's only race so it was easy to watch the competitors (they couldn't get away in a group of men). One girl did take off from the gun quickly but we had checked the competitors list beforehand and had marked who the likely winners were. The girl who had gone off in the lead was not on the list so although she was kept in

61

sight the main field were quite happy to let her go and as it turned out she was soon passed. The Americans had been favourites but as Joyce was a complete novice she was able to steal the show by breaking away and eventually coming home a comfortable winner in 2 hours 36 minutes 27 seconds. It proved that you should know who you are racing against.

*An early leader being caught by the chasing group in the Avon International marathon at Waldneil, West Germany.*

Race number three took us over to Tokyo. Having won the Avon race Joyce was now a 'known' marathon runner even though the Avon race had been only her second race, and in Tokyo Joyce went with the leaders. This race again was an all-women's race, with not many more than 50 runners but including the elite from all over the world. The course in Tokyo finishes up hill after a flat first 20 miles. At the drink station before the hill Joyce took her drink better than her rival at that point and pulled away from her by some 10 metres in the space of about 40 metres. Having gained the advantage, Joyce pushed the pace along which because of the up hill stretch did not enable her rival to catch up easily and again Joyce came home first in 2 hours 37 minutes 48 seconds. The practice Joyce had taken in drinking on the run during training proved very useful.

Race number four was a disaster for Joyce. It was in Miami on 12th January, 1980 and the race was run in high temperatures and humidity. Because it was a mass marathon, personal drinks could not be catered for so the runners had to rely on what the race organisers provided. The drink containers had been disinfected but left a peculiar taste, so Joyce instead of ignoring the nastiness went without and dehydrated, eventually collapsing with heat exhaustion. Joyce had learnt the hardest possible way to have every respect for the local weather conditions and she now takes drinks whenever it is warm.

Joyce's next major race was to have been the defence of her Avon Cosmetics International marathon title but after Miami she felt she needed another marathon to regain her confidence. The marathon at Sandbach on 22nd June, 1980 fell at a convenient time so Joyce went there for a 'training run'. That training run turned out to be quite different, the Swiss champion was in the race and wanted to break 2 hours 40 minutes. Joyce ran round with her and pulled away in the final two miles to finish in 2 hours 33 minutes 32 seconds for a British best performance in what had been a training run! However, Joyce now felt fully prepared for the defence of her Avon title.

The Avon Cosmetics International Marathon was to be held in London on 3rd August, 1980, it was Joyce's sixth marathon and for the first time ever the central streets of London were to be closed for a marathon race. However, fate was not on Joyce's side as five weeks before the race she caught chicken pox from Lisa, our eldest daughter. A week off because of that, back to training and then two weeks before the race a torn calf muscle stopped training again. Fortunately some excellent physiotherapy meant that only four days training was actually missed but training had to be gradually introduced after the injury. On reflection Joyce shouldn't really have started but this race was important for women's marathon running and Joyce lined up with the best in the world but during the race her calf muscle tightened up around the 20 miles point and Joyce had to take it easy into the finish. Joyce finished seventh, the first British athlete home, in 2 hours 41 minutes 22 seconds.

Race number seven was the defence of Joyce's Tokyo title on 16th November, 1980. Fortunately nothing went wrong in race preparations but it was necessary to work on speed endurance as the first part of the Tokyo course could be run fast but the hill at the end of the course would call upon athletes' strength. We knew training had gone well when Joyce ran a British best for 10 miles 5 weeks before the race and then ran the fastest leg in the Southern Counties road relay championships three weeks before. In Tokyo Joyce met up with Jackie Gareau of Canada and Allison Roe from New Zealand who had both run faster than Joyce and were hoping to break the $2\frac{1}{2}$-hours barrier. As we had thought likely the race was fast from the start especially with Jackie and Allison intent on trying for that $2\frac{1}{2}$-hours barrier. Fortunately Joyce was able to hold on to the pace and moved away on the hill near the finish. Joyce's time of 2 hours 30 minutes 27 seconds was a personal best and the fastest ever achieved in an all-women's race and also on an out-and-back course. The lessons were being learned and Joyce's training was proving to be right for her.

The London Marathon on 29th March, 1981 was Joyce's only marathon in 1981 and her second mass marathon. She didn't really expect to run a fast time as she had been running cross-country during the winter in which the longest distance she had raced was $3\frac{1}{2}$ miles. However being pulled along by the faster men and being surrounded by a fantastic crowd gave Joyce a tremendous feeling. The aches and pains were forgotten and another win in a British best of 2 hours 29 minutes 57 seconds was the result and elation at breaking the $2\frac{1}{2}$-hour barrier.

For the rest of 1981 Joyce was plagued with shin soreness, a pulling of the muscle along the shin bone, and when that was cured came the fight to regain fitness. An invitation came to run in Osaka on 24th January, 1982. Consequently that race was selected for Joyce's ninth ever marathon. Training didn't go according to plan for this marathon as Britain's weather took a turn for the worse and we experienced some of the heaviest snowfalls ever. Joyce carried on training but on one long run slipped on some ice and badly bruised her back which restricted training. Joyce was therefore pleased with her time of 2 hours 35 minutes 34 seconds but not with her placing, coming in fifth.

On to the defence of her London title and Joyce's tenth marathon on 9th May 1982. The training had gone to plan and Joyce was hopeful of a fast time. However the late entry into the race at the last moment of Lorraine Moller from New Zealand who was one place higher than Joyce on the all-time world ranking list and who had never lost a marathon race meant Joyce had to decide whether to run to win or go out for a fast time even though she may be beaten. After a steady start during the first 5 miles with both Joyce and Lorraine watching each other, Joyce picked up the pace but as in her very first race did so too quickly and consequently suffered in the final mile. Another factor ignored in this race was that the finish had been changed from the previous year and although Joyce knew the position of the finish line she was not acquainted with the run in over the final few miles, consequently she misjudged the miles to go over the latter part of the course. Even if a race is in your own back yard it pays to check every aspect as if it is in foreign territory.

## JOYCE SMITH'S MARATHON TABLE

*Race 1. Sandbach, Cheshire 2:41·36 1st*
   Poor pace judgement.

*Race 2. Waldneil, West Germany 2:36·27 1st*
   Ladies only races enables you to watch your rivals easily, be able to cover any breaks by other competitors.

*Race 3. Tokyo. 2:37·48 1st*
   Value in practice of drinking while running.

*Race 4. Miami.*
Take regard of weather need to drink when hot and humid.

*Race 5. Sandbach, Cheshire. 2:33·32 1st*
Confidence boosting race ran relaxed and fast.

*Race 6. Avon, London. 2:41·22 7th*
Should not have run after an illness and injury.

*Race 7. Tokyo. 2:30·27 1st*
Trained with known rivals in mind and planned race accordingly.

*Race 8. London. 2:29·57 1st*
Crowds and male runners can raise your performance – could make you run too fast also – noted for the future.

*Race 9. Osaka. 2:35·34 5th*
Ran after training was restricted by a fall in snow never expect your best performance after poor training.

*Race 10. London. 2:29·43 1st*
Check the course route, take note of pace and rivals, be prepared to abandon pre-race plans if necessary.

Planning ahead involves learning from the past and if you can do that successfully you can look forward to improvement in your running.

# Middle and long-distance running on the track

The distance races at any track meeting usually attract quite a bit of attention and at many an international meeting they have provided the highlight of the meeting. Such events, from the 800 metres upwards, are run with a great deal of interest for both competitor and spectator. Track athletes who compete in the distance events must have tactical ability, speed, endurance – and strength to bring their speed into play at the right time. These abilities will vary according to the distance being run – obviously the 800-metres runner will require more basic speed than the 10,000-metres runner. These differing basic requirements are reflected by the various styles of running. The faster the runner has to go, the greater the knee lift and the bigger the back kick, whereas the further a runner has to go, the greater the need for a more economical style and the knees do not come up so high and the back kick is kept to a minimum.

Most people find that the style of running comes naturally from the speed they run. It is not something that is normally practised by distance runners although if they are training to attain greater speed then emphasis is often placed on knee lift including lifting the hips. What is particularly aimed for in training is reproduction of the requirements of the particular event the athlete will race in.

*Joyce showing good 'drive' during a track race.*

At this point it is necessary to refer to two types of muscle action: *aerobic*, whereby the amount of oxygen used up by the muscles does not exceed the oxygen breathed in by the athlete, and *anaerobic* muscle action that requires greater amounts of oxygen than the body can supply, so the muscles work without oxygen and therefore go into oxygen debt. When this happens, your legs feel as though they are made of jelly, you may feel sick if you are not too fit and some time will elapse before breathing returns to normal. How these two muscle actions work in practice can be illustrated by jogging or running steadily over a distance of about 100 metres; the pace would be roughly that at which you would run a marathon. At the end of the 100 metres you should find no difference in your rate of breathing from when you first started. Now run the same distance at top speed and at the end of the 100 metres you will be gasping for breath and trying to gulp air into your body. Having run hard your muscles have been unable to obtain sufficient oxygen for the exertion and they have therefore gone into oxygen debt which has to be paid back afterwards. So we have these two types of muscle action, one with sufficient oxygen at the time and one without. Depending on the event you run you will need to use the two actions in different ratios. For instance in a 200-metres race, of the amount of oxygen required, only 5% is taken during the race and the body has an oxygen debt of 95%. In effect you would have only taken in a few gulps of air during the 200 metres but ask anyone how often they breathed in during a sprint race and invariably they won't remember. After the race comes the hard breathing during recovery.

Work done by the physiologist, A. V. Hill, shows the varying percentages for the different race distances:

| | Oxygen intake | Oxygen debt/ Oxygen reserve |
|---|---|---|
| *Race distance* | *Aerobic running* | *Anaerobic running* |
| 200 metres | 5% | 95% |
| 400 metres | 17% | 83% |
| 800 metres | 34% | 66% |

|  | **Oxygen intake** | **Oxygen debt/ Oxygen reserve** |
|---|---|---|
| 1500 metres | 50% | 50% |
| 5000 metres | 80% | 20% |
| 10,000 metres | 90% | 10% |
| Marathon | 98% | 2% |

Looking at the figures for 800-metres runners, they should learn to run 34% of their race by aerobic running – running while breathing regularly, and should train so that 66% of their run is anaerobic or speed running where the body goes into oxygen debt. On the other hand 10,000 metres runners will spend their training time doing 90% aerobic running and 10% devoted to anaerobic work.

Long-distance runs represent aerobic runs while repetition running, an example of which might be four to six 400 metres at 800-metres pace with a suitable rest in between, represent anaerobic training. Further examples will be given later. The chapter on athletics for women gives details of the physiological differences between male and female athletes and this must be borne in mind when considering middle-distance training for women. Because of the lower oxygen carrying capacity of women compared to men, the aerobic training for women in the middle distance events should be slightly more than the figures given in the table. Women running 800-metres races should have an approximate ratio of 50% aerobic and 50% anaerobic work in their training, while 1500-metres runners could train in the ratio of 60% aerobic 40% anaerobic. Looked at in another way there is the same muscle/oxygen requirement in the female athlete's 2 minutes/800 metres which is a good time for a woman, and a good male athlete's 1-mile pace as they are training in the ratio of 50% aerobic 50% anaerobic.

This variation in training for women became apparent to us during the winter of 1966. That winter Joyce was training for cross-country races and during that season finished 2nd in both the Southern and National Cross-Country Championships. Joyce also ran in the

W.A.A.A. 1 mile indoor championships which she won in 5 minutes 3·6 seconds, the best time ever recorded then for a mile indoors. Later in the winter season of 1971 Margaret Beacham who was training at that time with Joyce and was doing more aerobic work than anaerobic, was European 1500 metres indoor champion and holder of the world best for women over 1500 metres indoors. All this was achieved during the winter and with very little track work.

Having stated the need to find the right balance in training between steady running and speed work there are different ways in which this can be achieved. Coaches have come up with different training ideas so that there is no monotony in training. A brief description of the most common types of training used in distance running is given below to help you understand the jargon used in the running world.

**Steady running**     This is exactly what it says: running at a steady even pace without any breathing difficulties. If running with a partner you could talk easily at this pace. This is the simplest form of aerobic training.

**L.S.D. or Long slow (steady) distance**     An American-derived training method where the runner may run for 2 or 3 hours at a slower than usual pace. What is lacking in quality is made up by quantity in this type of training.

**Fartlek**     A Swedish word meaning speed play. The runner accomplishes a distance run over a period which could range from 30 to 60 minutes. During the run the runner would change pace as he or she felt able. For instance there could be 600 metres of easy running, followed by a 100-metres sprint then 200 metres easy then 400 metres at a fast stride followed by 800 metres easy. Running this way in Swedish pine forests would be a very pleasant and exhilarating method of training. Basically aerobic with some anaerobic work thrown in.

**Repetition runs**     Generally carried out on the track but can be done equally successfully on the road or on grass. The runner or coach decides on a particular distance to run and will run a set number of repeats with sufficient rest between to ensure they are all run at the same speed. Generally the rest is sufficient to give almost full recovery, it is certainly enough to enable breathing to come back to normal. An example of repetition runs might be 6 times 400 metres with 400-metres walk rest in between. This is anaerobic training.

**Interval training**     Often mistaken as repetition running. In this type of training the interval or the period is important – it is kept to a minimum so that the athlete is not fully recovered before starting a fast effort run again. When this type of training first came out the interval (or rest!) period was the time taken for the pulse rate to drop down to 120 beats per second. This type of training is for the very fit athlete as it is training the heart and circulation to operate at higher capacity.

Variations in training are numerous and the more variety that can be introduced the greater the enjoyment for the runner. Steady running can be done over different routes and on different surfaces but uneven surfaces should be avoided. Running in sand provides a resistance for the runner and strengthens up the muscles involved in the running action, in the same way as hill running makes the runner work against gravity and increases leg strength. If there are no hills in the area which the runner trains over, then acceleration runs can provide a different type of training. In these runs a set distance is divided into 3 or 4 parts by markers and as the runner passes a marker he or she accelerates so that over the final part of the run the athlete is going flat out. Another alternative to the acceleration runs is the differential run. This could be done instead of a repetition run session, the distance to be run is divided in half and the first half run slower than the second half. For instance, if the distance to be run is 400 metres in 68 seconds, the first part might be run in 35 seconds and the second 200 metres run in 33 seconds. This type of training would also teach pace judgement and prepare athletes for a stronger finish.

One way a coach may teach athletes pace judgement is to set a distance which would be broken into equal sections and a whistle would be blown to let the athletes know they are on the right pace for the distance to be run. Supposing a 400 metres had to be run in 64 seconds then a whistle at every 16 seconds would indicate to the athlete that he or she would have to be passing the 300-metres point, the 200-metres point and 100-metres point as the whistle sounded.

So far the training mentioned has involved running, and while that is certainly the best way to train for running, the runner who is aiming to compete over 800 metres and 1500 metres especially should think of being as fully equipped as possible in physical makeup for competition. Weight training and circuit training should be considered for inclusion in the training schedule. The aim of these two types of training is to help increase areas of fitness where strength and strength endurance is required. Weight training needs to be supervised by a qualified coach. The number of injuries that have been caused by athletes weight training by themselves or incorrectly teaches the lesson of being wise after the event. So often an athlete will think a weight is light, and so it may be if the athlete is fresh, but after several exercises an athlete's strength is not what it was and after all that is exactly what we are trying to improve – strength during tiredness. For safety reasons weight training must only be done in pairs and only then when there is a qualified person present. Despite this reservation though there is one kind of weight training which can be done by the individual at home. The athlete is aiming to increase strength/body weight ratio and what better way to do it than to support your own body weight? Press ups, pull ups and sit ups can all be done safely and will prove to be beneficial.

Circuit training is a series of exercises done in a fixed rota with a pre-set number of repeats and each circuit of exercises is done 3 times. There might be 6 or 8 exercises in each circuit and the athlete performs these exercises after

*Alberto Juantarena, Olympic double-gold medallist, a strong and powerful runner.*

being previously tested on the various exercises. Generally he or she would do half their maximum on each circuit of exercises. Progress would be measured by reducing the time taken to complete the 3 circuits or by increasing the repetitions of the various exercises. There is no reason why an athlete should not complete a mini circuit in the home, training does not have to be done in the gymnasium.

Like the gardener who prepares his ground, sows his seeds then feeds and waters them for a good showing so the athlete prepares him or herself in preparation for competition. The weight training or circuit training are adding strength, the steady runs add to endurance, exercises increase mobility. Then, just before the competition period, comes the sharpening up with speed work which aims to produce an athlete raring for races.

To illustrate the build up and preparation here are some examples of the training to be done at different times of the year for the various distances. The schedules are very general and what a club athlete might be doing. People can of course train on their own and work out their own schedules which suit them better.

## THE 800-METRES RUNNER

These runners fall into 3 categories, assuming that the main racing season is in the summer months:
(a) those that run cross-country races,
(b) those that race indoors,
(c) those that do neither (a) or (b) above but train for the summer and perhaps take part in another sport like football or hockey.

The cross-country runner could follow the cross-country training mentioned in the next chapter, but generally a man would have to decide whether he was really suited to run 9 miles cross-country as is required in the major championships; he may well be content to run in the club 5-mile races which fill up the club fixture list. The female runner has no need to worry about the longer distances as most women's cross-country races do not generally exceed 3½ miles and many a successful female 800-metres runner has run well in cross-country races. The indoor racers would take a break in September or October depending on their summer racing programme and then start building up their endurance by aerobic training and also bring in weight training/circuit training. A typical week's training for the 800-metres runner in October/November might be as follows:

| | |
|---|---|
| SUNDAY | long run up to 8 miles |
| MONDAY | circuit training/weight training |
| TUESDAY | track session |
| WEDNESDAY | even paced run up to 8 miles. |
| THURSDAY | hill running – repetition sprints up hill |
| FRIDAY | rest |
| SATURDAY | fartlek running or participation in a team sport |

In January the indoor runner would increase the speed running sessions, Saturday's training would become a track running session as might Thursday's training and on Monday the circuit training or weight training may end with an even-paced race or be preceded by a very good warm-up run. A word of warning – track training in the winter will mean running fast and slow in the cold weather, it is therefore essential that runners keep themselves warm all of the time, if necessary by training in a track suit.

The runner referred to in (c), the 'non-running runner', should be very much concerned with keeping fit and would include a variety of running on different days in the winter. There may be some club training evenings if the athlete belongs to a hockey, rugby or football club. To do nothing all winter would make it difficult to maintain a state of fitness that would enable any progression to take place the following year.

In the spring the 800-metres runner should be busy preparing for the track season that lies ahead. A typical week's training may be as follows:

| | |
|---|---|
| SUNDAY | track session |
| MONDAY | steady running about 6 miles |

*Indoor racing. Note the angle of the runners on the camber.*

TUESDAY      track session
WEDNESDAY steady running for 5 miles
THURSDAY   hill climbs or sand running
FRIDAY         rest
SATURDAY    fartlek running on grassland

In the main competition period the athlete will probably be racing on some Saturdays depending on the demands of the club or how often the individual likes to race. Just because we have been talking about the 800-metres runner doesn't mean that the athlete will always be competing at that particular distance. Races at 400 metres and perhaps occasionally at 200 metres and 1500 metres would vary the programme. A week's training at competition time might be arranged as:

SUNDAY       steady run of 6 miles aerobic run
MONDAY       fartlek run on grassland
TUESDAY      track training
WEDNESDAY steady run up to 5 miles
THURSDAY   track session

77

FRIDAY rest

SATURDAY race.

Track sessions can be as varied as the coach or athlete likes to make them. In the winter emphasis would be placed on the endurance and strengthening side of an athlete's build up. Consequently the track sessions might be 3 times 600 metres or 10 times 400 metres, perhaps 10 seconds slower than race pace but with a short recovery time. As the athlete approaches the competition season so the number of repetition runs will decrease or the distance of the effort will drop but everything should be run faster. Sessions might include 6 times 400 metres at 800-metres race pace, with 400-metres walk or slow jog rest or 8 times 200 metres with 200-metres walk rest.

## THE 1500-METRES RUNNER

While the 800-metres runner may be described as a speed runner with some endurance ability the 1500-metres runner could be described as an endurance runner with some speed ability. Many of Britain's top 1500-metres runners have competed with distinction in cross-country races and many train in the winter for the cross-country season. The 1500-metres runner can therefore follow a cross-country training programme during the winter, but for those people who do not like to race over the country indoor racing is possible. Indeed some runners have managed to combine cross-country racing and indoor running thereby increasing the variety open to them.

For the 1500-metres runner wishing to compete indoors the early winter season training may go as follows:

SUNDAY 10 miles run

MONDAY circuit training and 5 miles run

TUESDAY track session which might be 4 times 800 metres with 400 metres jog recovery

WEDNESDAY 8 miles run or 5 miles fartlek

THURSDAY hill running or track session

FRIDAY rest

78

*A 1500-metre race. Joyce leads and has no worries about possibilities of tripping up, unlike one or two of the closely bunched runners behind.*

SATURDAY    fartlek running or club cross-country
race

In January the hill running would be replaced by a track session as might the Saturday cross-country race or fartlek session. Then as the athletes get closer to the competition period so they would increase the speed of the sessions. As I mentioned before, while track training in the winter, runners must beware of getting cold as this can lead to pulled muscles.

The spring will see the 1500-metres runner, like most other track and field athletes, getting ready for the summer competition period ahead. Working on the 50% aerobic training and 50% anaerobic training break-down, the male 1500-metres runner would consider doing 3 speed sessions and 3 endurance runs per week. The female 1500-metres runner might divide her training into 2 speed sessions (anaerobic) and 4 endurance runs (aerobic). The international athlete by the way could well be running 10 to 14 sessions per week!

In the main competition period, the 1500-metres runner like the 800-metres runner, will probably race at distances either side of his or her main distance, racing over 800 metres and 3000 metres. It would be rare to find an athlete who sticks to just the one distance for racing. Often a runner is an 800/1500 metres runner or a 1500/3000 metres runner. Whatever the case, the training would be geared accordingly. In the first case more emphasis might be placed on speed work while in the latter case more stress should be placed on endurance.

The endurance runs for this group of runners would involve steady running on the road or over grassland ranging from 6 miles to 12 miles and if this is done with other runners and over different courses it is a very enjoyable way of training. Track sessions can vary enormously and a small sample of different sessions are given below:

10 or 12 × 400 metres with a 200 metres jog rest
8 × 300 metres faster than 800 metres race pace, with 5 minutes rest
4 × 600 metres with 600 metres jog/walk recovery
16 × 200 metres with 100 metres jog recovery
3 × 800 metres with 800 metres jog recovery
2 × 1000 metres with 10 minutes rest
10 × 150 metres flat out with walk back recovery

Then there are variations on the above such as:

4 × 300 metres followed by 5 × 150 metres or
1 × 1000 metres followed by 6 × 200 metres

Should the athlete want a change from running around the track these sessions can be done on grass. During the summer of 1974 when Joyce was preparing for the European Championships many of her track sessions were done around the boundary of the local cricket field. Most cricket boundaries are around 400 metres but if times are taken they must only be compared with previous times around the same course. An alternative to running set distances is to run a marked course, such as a track or cricket boundary, for a set time – say 2 minutes. The runner then repeats this, perhaps 3 times, and aims to achieve the same distance or a little bit more each time.

*A mile race at White City on a cinder track. Ann Smith (10) shows good tactical positioning.*

## THE 3000-METRES RUNNER

3000 metres is a useful distance for the male athlete. The 1500-metres runner moves up to 3000 metres, in order to race over his main distance, thereby testing his endurance. The 5000-metres and 10,000-metres runners move down to experience a faster than race pace speed. However for the female athlete this is a championship distance and therefore one which many women concentrate on.

During the winter the athletes concentrating on 3000 metres will invariably race cross-country although they can also run indoors at this distance. The winter training will be the same as that for the cross-country runner although some 1500-metres runners may race the 3000 distance indoors. The training breakdown for this event is approximately 30% anaerobic and 70% aerobic, although the female athlete would probably benefit with a 20% anaerobic 80% aerobic breakdown. This would mean a woman running long runs 4 times to 1 session speed work on the track. Up until now we have not been talking about the speed of the long runs. The 3000-metres runner would certainly vary the pace of the long runs, for example 3 miles could be done fast, so there would be some anaerobic element while 12 miles would be done at a very easy pace at which you could talk to any companions with you.

Because of the longer distance to be raced the track sessions would correspondingly be extended, for instance:

15 × 400 metres at race pace or
5 × 800 metres or
3 × 1200 metres.

Similarly the long runs would be extended. In fact the 3000-metres track runner could easily switch to a short road race if he or she desired and likewise could easily move up to run 5000 metres on the track.

## THE 5000-METRES AND 10,000-METRES TRACK RUNNER

I have bracketed the two distances together mainly because the opportunities to race 10,000 metres on the track are not very frequent. Nor would a runner want to run the distance too often because, like the marathon, to race 10,000 metres well a considerable amount of preparation and a recovery period are required. The male 5000-metres runner has more racing opportunities than the 10,000-metres runner and would be running two speed sessions in training, which may be on the track, to eight distance runs. He will certainly be a cross-country runner in the winter and may occasionally have a run in some road races. During track training the types of sessions might be:

6 to 8 × 800 metres
15 to 20 × 400 metres
3 or 4 × 1 mile or 1600 metres.

A good fartlek session of 8 miles with the emphasis on long efforts of perhaps 1 mile or more would be beneficial.

*Tony Simmons leads Brendan Foster and Julian Goater in a 5000-metre race.*

However while the distance of the race requires endurance, many a race is won on a sprint finish, so it would benefit the 5000-metres runner to run some track sessions with the 1500-metres runners.

The 10,000 metres is an event which an athlete may only be called upon to run once or twice during a season, so invariably if a 10,000-metres race is fitted into the athlete's racing programme the schedule would be arranged so that there is a build-up to the day of that event. So for around 6 weeks prior to the 10,000 metres, the athlete who would already have been following a fairly hard training programme, would be practising pace judgement and getting used to running 25 laps around the track. This would be done by repetition runs on the track as described above for the 5000-metres runner but much of the work would be done on the road, running distances from 6 to 18 miles.

## TRACK TRAINING HINTS

When Joyce was training for track races she never wore spiked shoes unless it was for a time trial (when the athlete will aim to run a set distance in a set time) or unless she was doing specific speed work. Therefore all her track sessions were done in road training shoes which were heavier than spikes and did not give the grip that spikes would give. The reasons for this were that when spikes were put on they felt light and therefore gave a psychological boost that Joyce had an advantage to race in. Also without spikes in training Joyce had to work harder. Much of her training was done on cinder tracks before the advent of all-weather tracks. Some rivals could run better track sessions than Joyce but couldn't beat her when it came to racing. What they didn't realize is that they wore spikes for training while Joyce did not. Nowadays, with synthetic tracks, there is almost no need to train in spikes for distance events and more robust training shoes give better protection to the athlete and could reduce injury risks.

Train in comfort. Firstly, keep warm. Don't strip down to vests and shorts to run a fast training session if it means a risk of a pulled muscle. A pair of woollen tights or thermal underwear are invaluable aids on a cold winter night. Far better to complete a training session in slower times than limp home after pulling a muscle and have to miss a week's training. Train don't strain is a saying often

*Joyce relaxes in the lead of a 3000-metre race at Crystal Palace, but she keeps on running undistracted by the commotion near the tape.*

85

heard. Some athletes seem to think every training session is a race and although they are first past the finish post in every training run they cannot understand when they do not win races. Often the reason is that they left their competitive spirit on the training track. Training should be hard but after a shower you should be looking forward to tomorrow's session. Don't run yourself stale. You are meant to be doing it for enjoyment.

When it comes to racing, tactics are very important. When do you take to lead? Is it from the gun or in the last 50 metres? So often the answer will depend upon who you are racing against. Don't be fooled by a person's basic speed – by that I mean the speed at which a person can run 100 or 200 metres. In one 3000 metres race at Crystal Palace, Joyce, who was returning after injury, was running against athletes who had much faster 800, 400 and 200-metres times than her, yet when it came to the last 200 metres and there was still a bunch together it was Joyce who managed to sprint away to win. The other runners were running close to their best pace for the distance of the race while Joyce still felt comfortable and because of her greater speed endurance was able to raise her pace at the end faster than her rivals. It is therefore wise when looking at your rivals to find out what they can do at the end of a distance race rather than what their best 200-metres time is. If, however, the race if very slow then the person with better basic speed will have an advantage.

There are therefore occasions when it is worth leading in order to try and run the finishing sprint out of your rivals. Sometimes there are runners who like to lead, it gives them confidence and they consequently run well when doing so. While it may be relaxing to run behind another runner it could upset a natural leader if you take the lead from him or her.

Being able to successfully accomplish pre-arranged tactics can be very satisfying. Successful tactics surprise your rivals by catching them unaware because prior to the race they will have decided upon a tactic to beat you.

# Cross-country running

Cross-country running is a popular form of winter racing for the distance runners and throughout Britain races are held every weekend. Many of Britain's running clubs started as cross-country or harrier clubs and developed later into track and field clubs. The cross-country season starts in October and goes through to March, culminating with the National Cross-Country Championships which are open to teams from every affiliated club. From the National Championships teams are selected to represent their country in the International Cross-Country Championships which are held every year and are organised by the world's ruling athletic body, the International Amateur Athletic Federation.

Cross-country running is open to everyone and a novice athlete could find him or herself standing next to an international on the starting line of an inter-club fixture. Everyone's performance is important in the race because of the team competition that is generally held within most races. The team scoring is calculated by giving the first runner home in the race 1 point, the second home 2 points and so on. Each team would score their first 4, 6, or sometimes 8 runners and the team with the lowest score would be declared the winners. Consider the following possible team scoring:

| Team A | Team B | Team C |
|:------:|:------:|:------:|
| 2 | 4 | 1 |
| 3 | 6 | 5 |
| 8 | 7 | 9 |
| 15 | 10 | 13 |
| 28 | 27 | 28 |
| 16 | 11 | 14 |
| 17 | 12 | 18 |

Team B is the winning team because they have the lowest score, team C is second because although they had the same score as team A their last scorer passed the finishing line before team A's last scorer (this is the method used to decide a tie on points). The importance of every runner can be seen: if Team B's fifth and sixth runner had not beaten teams A and C's fourth runner then team B would not have won. If team C's fourth runner had not beaten team A's fourth runner, team C would not have been second. It is therefore important for cross-country runners to remember that everyone is important in the team competition, not just the scoring members of the team, or those individuals leading the race. Sometimes it is the non-scoring members who could win the race for their team.

Cross-country races can be run over a wide range of courses. Some could be parkland with short cut grass, therefore making it a fast running course. At the other extreme, the course could be muddy and hilly, providing a test of strength and stamina for the runner. There could be obstacles to negotiate like streams, stiles, fences and fallen trees. The course could be over parkland, in woods, over ploughed fields, up and down hills or on relatively flat ground. While the ground could be dry or wet, muddy or grass, firm or soft, all in all the variety that a cross-country course can provide gives a challenge in addition to the competition that breeds good distance runners.

The distances of races vary throughout the cross-country season. For men's relays the range might be from relay legs of 2 miles in distance so that the race could be 6 legs of 2 miles, to the 9 miles of area and national championships. Younger age groups would compete over a

*Cross-country races can be on mud or grassland. You will need to be prepared for all conditions.*

shorter distance. At championship level the distance would be 6 miles for those under 20, 4 miles for the under 17s and 3 miles for runners under 15. The ladies' distances are considerably shorter in the championships. They would run over courses of approximately the following distances: under 13s – $1\frac{3}{4}$ miles, under 15s – 2 miles, under 17s – $2\frac{1}{2}$ miles, and over 17 – $3\frac{1}{2}$ miles. Many club races for senior men will be over a 5-mile course and for senior ladies $2\frac{1}{2}$ miles during the cross-country season.

Training for cross-country racing must cater for many variations because of the different types of courses and differing distances the runner may face. Generally, training during the cross-country season will be done on

89

the road, but what must be remembered is that the firmer surface of the road makes it much easier to run over than the softer surface offered by many cross-country courses, because the softer surface absorbs some of the driving power of the runner's action. This can of course be to the advantage of the runner by strengthening the leg muscles of the runner and reducing the continual pounding the legs might otherwise suffer on a hard surface. If you can train on grass during the winter it is beneficial, but often runners have to train after dusk, and it is far better to run on a lit hard surface such as a road surface than run on unlit grass which could be uneven thus risking injury.

One of the aspects that the cross-country runner will find on both road and country are hills and therefore hill training on the road can prove beneficial when running up hills in the country. When training on hills remember that it is important to continue running over the brow of the hill. In Joyce's early cross-country days one of her rivals used to run hard up the hills but was always caught just after the top of the hill. We found out the reason for this when watching one of the club training sessions. The athletes would repeatedly sprint up a hill but stop at the top of the hill or just before the top. This was obviously being carried over in the race so that all the advantage of being first to the top of the hill was immediately being lost. So often a hard run over the top of a hill will have more effect than sprinting up a hill. There is also a psychological advantage to be gained in some cases by continuing to run hard over a hill and down the other side. If a runner is leading others by a small distance when going up hill and that distance is say 10 metres, the leading runner when freewheeling down the hill will appear to have gained perhaps 5 extra metres when the others reach the top of the hill. They are then under the impression that the leader is full of running and moving away from them. The same effect can be gained on courses with sharp corners. The leading runner can gain advantage by striding away hard after turning a corner thereby gaining ground on opponents and perhaps the move will deter them from trying to catch him or her. The move will work in any situation where one runner has a narrow lead over another which is often the case when a cross country or road race is spread out. The counter move to such a tactic is to stride hard after your opponent. When he or she turns a corner so that when he or she looks round again after turning you seem closer and give the impression you are catching up.

Such tactics will need to be practised in training and during a training run you may urge yourself to sprint hard for 100 metres after turning a corner or alternatively sprint hard to a corner. Because of the varying nature of cross-country races it is important to vary training during the cross-country season. What must be remembered is that during a cross-country race pace can vary all the time and the runner would be experiencing different degrees of aerobic and anaerobic running (see page 69). For instance, going uphill the runner could be breathing heavily because of the greater exertion and would go into oxygen debt. But when running downhill the athlete could be

*Hill running, an important factor in cross-country.*

91

doing easy aerobic running whereby gravity is doing the work and the runner may repay some of the oxygen debt incurred during the race. I don't want to give the impression that in cross-country races you must run hard uphill and easy downhill. The object of the race is to complete the whole distance as quickly as possible and the runner must decide what is the best way to do that after seeing the course.

Generally most cross-country runners are track or road athletes as well as 'country' competitors and after the track season it is best to have an easy period as a transition before cross-country running. This is not necessarily always the case, if an athlete has been injured in the track

*Coming downhill but keeping an eye on your rivals.*

*Going round the corner onto the flat, take up a good racing position so that no one can break away.*

season and forced to rest from running there would be no advantage in taking a rest at the end of the track season just because it is custom to do so. The injured athlete should be aiming to get back to full fitness.

Having finished a track season most runners will have to consider the building up of endurance and strength for the coming cross-country racing season so they will be preparing in November and December for the main events in the cross-country calendar which come after Christmas. This is not to say they will not be racing in the preparatory period, there are plenty of club races for them to compete in. Indeed racing over varying distances can provide a valuable guide to how much progress is being made in training. Whereas during the track season, the emphasis will have been on speed work especially so for the 800 metres and 1500-metres runners, the emphasis now shifts to endurance. The track runner must not look upon the winter season as a cross-country season that is just providing an alternative racing programme so that he or she can continue with the sport. The winter season is also a time of building up ready for the next summer. The build up for the long runs should be done slowly by adding a little bit extra each week. A sample week's training during this period might be as set out below:

| | |
|---|---|
| SUNDAY | long run building up to between 12 to 20 miles for men and 8 to 12 miles for women |
| MONDAY | circuit training or a fast 4 × 6 miles road run |
| TUESDAY | track training could vary from 6 × 400 metres for young athletes with 400 metres jog recovery to 8 × 800 metres with 400 metres jog for senior men |
| WEDNESDAY | long run varying between 8 to 15 miles |
| THURSDAY | run of 3 to 7 miles or 3 × 2 miles fast runs on the road |
| FRIDAY | rest |
| SATURDAY | race or cross-country fartlek session |

Training schedules or programmes will vary so much that it is very difficult to generalise. Obviously a 13-year-old girl would not follow the above programme nor would a person just starting out in athletic training. Distances and speed of runs vary because of the lengths of the different cross-country races for men and women in their different age classifications. Some runners may only be training twice or three times a week whereas an international athlete could be training twice a day on some days, perhaps on every day in a few cases. The track sessions are the hardest to give guidance for because they must suit the individual. There are so many variations not only as to the distance being run, but also in the speed of the run and the distance and speed of the recovery.

The cross-country runner must learn to accept any type of course. What has to be remembered all of the time is that everyone in the race competes over the same course and

*Young cross-country runners just after the start.*

the hills are just as steep for the front runners as those at the back. If you allow yourself to be put off by one particular aspect, such as hills, then you invariably will not run well. If you become aware of a weakness, then rectify it in training. We have heard athletes say after seeing a course for the first time, "I'm not going to run well today, the course is too hilly, muddy, flat, short, etc." If they have that opinion then their training is wrong as well as their racing attitude. If athletes don't like hills then they should make a particular point of training on hills, if they don't like mud, spend some weekends looking for muddy ground to run over. They should learn how to run over mud, try running with different actions, try shorter strides or longer strides, try leaning forward or running more upright. In training you can experiment and by experimenting you will learn what is right for you.

The question of what happens when you turn up for a cross-country race will be dealt with later in the chapter on the day of the race, but it is worth finding out in advance what a particular course is like or if a certain competition is different from others. For instance the International Cross-Country Championships now have hurdles put around the course as extra obstacles. The taking of obstacles causes an interruption in the running action which if you are not used to it can be quite a distraction in the race.

As I mentioned in the last chapter, about track running, Joyce never trained on the track in spikes unless it was for a time trial or a speed session. It is not always possible to train over the country in training or flat shoes because you could spend much time slipping and sliding which could cause injury. If the area you are training over looks as though it could cause you to slip, play safe and put your spikes on. Such an occasion gives you a good opportunity to try out different lengths of screw-in spikes.

*Make sure your spikes are long enough to grip the ground without tripping up, but not too short to be covered by mud.*

Cross-country runners will soon find out that they are not confined to running over country terrain in straight races. If they are club members, at some time a club official will ask them to compete for the club in a cross-country relay or a road relay. These relays have proved to be a very popular area of competition. Teams vary from 3 to 12, and each member of the team will run around a set course, usually doing 2 or 3 miles before handing over to a team mate who will run the same course. Batons are generally not used and the incoming runner usually touches the hand of the outgoing runner for a legal change over. Many runners find these relay races an enjoyable and relaxing way of racing because success depends on team effort. Road relays can vary by having different length distances which a runner has to complete and instead of completing a circuit the race could be a relay from point A to point B.

*Steve Ovett (322) leads the National Cross-Country Championship field at the start.*

Road relays often provide an introduction to road racing for many a cross-country runner but road running can be done through the year and that is what we are going to discuss next.

# Road runner

For the person who wants to be a distance runner, road running provides every possibility. Road running (for training purposes we mean pavement running) provides a firm even surface to train and race over. In the dark winter evenings street lighting ensures the runner can still see where he or she is running and there are no restrictions to the time you can use the road. Running tracks and parks have closing times and there is a fee to use running tracks but the freedom of the road is very apparent to the road runner.

Road races vary from short road races, usually 5 miles, to ultra-distance races like the London to Brighton road race which is $53\frac{1}{2}$ miles, but for most road runners the marathon is the longest distance they might aim to compete over. Probably the two most popular distances for road races in Britain are 10 miles and marathon but races can be found over most distances measured in miles and kilometres. The race organiser should have ensured that the course has been measured accurately and although you can compare times over courses over the same distance you should always remember courses can vary as can the weather so you cannot compare a 10 miles over a hilly course on a windy day to a 10 miles on a flat course on a pleasant cool day. However it is surprising how many of the top runners will turn out similar times on various courses so if you are running consistently you will find that your times fall within a certain range and another guide will be your position against fellow runners. Your time behind the winner or how your time compares with runners you have competed against before provides talking points for the after-race analysis.

In the schedules the type of running has been varied and the definition of the different terms for types of running is:

**Jog**    short strides, relaxed, you should be able to hold a conversation very easily with a companion, there is no aim to run fast, it is just faster than good walking pace.

**Easy running**    the next stage up from jogging, a slightly longer stride but you should still be able to breathe easily, never getting out of breath. Warming up pace.

**Steady running**    even-paced running throughout the session, it will feel easy at first but as you tire, so it will make you breathe harder. The speed of running throughout will depend on your fitness.

**Hard or fast running**    top speed running, almost race pace requiring maximum concentration, no time for talking in these sessions.

If run is stated then the athlete has a choice. Obviously he or she cannot do hard running every day but equally should not do easy running every day. Finding the right balance will vary from individual to individual, it is no good doing 2 consecutive hard runs and then not being able to train for the next 3 days because you are too tired. However, a day's rest if things have really got on top of you is more beneficial than slogging out another session.

The schedule set out below is aimed at providing guidance for those who have never competed but are keen to have a go at road running and would like to run a marathon. The marathon is after all a test not just against your fellow competitors but for you as an individual to be able to complete the distance is an achievement; to im-

*Easy running means you can talk to a companion, here Joyce and Ingrid Kristiansen are running easy in a marathon race.*

prove your time next time out is an even greater achievement. *In addition to the time spent on the road running and walking don't forget your exercises* (see Chapter 3).

## A SIX MONTH TRAINING PLAN TOWARDS THE MARATHON FOR THE COMPLETE BEGINNER

**Week 1.**

Sunday:     15 minutes jog/walk
Monday:     rest
Tuesday:    15 minutes jog/walk

Wednesday: rest
Thursday:   15 minutes jog/walk
Friday & Saturday: rest

**Week 2.**
Sunday:       10 minutes jog
Monday:       rest
Tuesday:      20 minutes jog/walk
Wednesday: 10 minutes jog
Thursday:     20 minutes walk
Friday & Saturday: rest

**Week 3.**
Sunday:       15 minutes jog
Monday:       rest
Tuesday:      25 minutes jog/walk
Wednesday: 10 minutes jog
Thursday:     25 minutes walk
Friday:       rest
Saturday:     15 minutes walk

**Week 4.**
Sunday:       20 minutes jog
Monday:       20 minutes walk
Tuesday:      15 minutes jog
Wednesday: 30 minutes walk
Thursday:     25 minutes jog/walk
Friday & Saturday: rest

**Week 5.**
Sunday:       25 minutes jog
Monday:       40 minutes walk
Tuesday:      20 minutes jog
Wednesday: 30 minutes jog
Thursday:     15 minutes jog
Friday:       20 minutes walk
Saturday:     rest

**Week 6.**
Sunday:       4 miles run
Monday:       rest
Tuesday:      20 minutes jog
Wednesday: 40 minutes jog
Thursday:     45 minutes jog/walk
Friday:       rest
Saturday:     40 minutes jog/walk

**Week 7.**
Sunday:       4 miles run
Monday:       1 hour walk
Tuesday:      3 miles run
Wednesday: 1 hour jog/walk
Thursday:     4 miles run

Friday:       4 miles run
Saturday:     rest

**Week 8.**
Sunday:       6 miles run
Monday:       1¼ hours walk
Tuesday:      3 miles run
Wednesday: 4 miles run
Thursday:     4 miles run
Friday:       rest
Saturday:     6 miles run

**Week 9.**
Sunday:       5 miles run
Monday:       3 miles run
Tuesday:      1½ hours walk
Wednesday: 8 miles run
Thursday:     1½ hours walk
Friday:       5 miles run
Saturday:     rest

**Week 10.**
Sunday:       6 miles run
Monday:       8 miles run
Tuesday:      3 miles run
Wednesday: 5 miles run
Thursday:     6 miles run
Friday:       4 miles run
Saturday:     3 miles run
*weekly mileage 35 miles*

**Week 11.**
Sunday:       8 miles run
Monday:       3 miles run
Tuesday:      5 miles run
Wednesday: 8 miles run
Thursday:     5 miles run
Friday:       rest
Saturday:     10 miles run
*weekly mileage 39 miles*

**Week 12.**
Sunday:       6 miles run
Monday:       4 miles run
Tuesday:      5 miles run
Wednesday: 8 miles run
Thursday:     5 miles run
Friday:       rest
Saturday:     6 miles run
*weekly mileage 34 miles*

**Week 13.**
Sunday: 10 miles run
Monday: 4 miles run
Tuesday: 6 miles run
Wednesday: 10 miles run
Thursday: 6 miles run
Friday: 4 miles run
Saturday: 8 miles run
*weekly mileage 48 miles*

**Week 14.**
Sunday: 12 miles run
Monday: 8 miles run
Tuesday: 8 miles run
Wednesday: 6 miles run
Thursday: 3 miles run
Friday: rest
Saturday: *race over 10
kilometres or 5 miles*
*weekly mileage 44 miles*

**Week 15.**
Sunday: 10 miles run
Monday: 6 miles run
Tuesday: 8 miles run
Wednesday: 10 miles run
Thursday: 6 miles run
Friday: 4 miles run
Saturday: 8 miles run
*weekly mileage 52 miles*

**Week 16.**
Sunday: 15 miles run
Monday: 8 miles run
Tuesday: 6 miles run
Wednesday: 12 miles run
Thursday: 6 miles run
Friday: rest
Saturday: 10 miles run
*weekly mileage 57 miles*

**Week 17.**
Sunday: 12 miles run
Monday: 6 miles run
Tuesday: 8 miles run
Wednesday: 15 miles run
Thursday: 8 miles run
Friday: 4 miles run
Saturday: rest
*weekly mileage 53 miles*

**Week 18.**
Sunday: 18 miles run
Monday: 8 miles run
Tuesday: 6 miles run
Wednesday: rest
Thursday: 12 miles run
Friday: 6 miles run
Saturday: rest
*weekly mileage 50 miles*

**Week 19.**
Sunday: 15 miles run
Monday: 8 miles run
Tuesday: 10 miles run
Wednesday: 12 miles run
Thursday: 8 miles run
Friday: rest
Saturday: 10 miles run
*weekly mileage 63 miles*

**Week 20.**
Sunday: 20 miles run
Monday: 8 miles run
Tuesday: 6 miles run
Wednesday: 12 miles run
Thursday: 8 miles run
Friday: 4 miles run at a
good pace
Saturday: 10 miles run
*weekly mileage 68 miles*

**Week 21.**
Sunday: 15 miles run
Monday: 10 miles run
Tuesday: 5 miles run
Wednesday: 8 miles run
Thursday: 6 miles run
Friday: rest
Saturday: *20 kilometres or
10 miles race*
*weekly mileage 55 miles*

**Week 22.**
Sunday: 12 miles run
very easy
Monday: 8 miles run
Tuesday: 6 miles run
Wednesday: 10 miles run
Thursday: 8 miles run

103

Friday:      6 miles run
Saturday:    rest
*weekly mileage 50 miles*

**Week 23.**
Sunday:      23 miles very easy
             run or run for
             period of time you
             expect to complete
             marathon in
Monday:      6 miles run
Tuesday:     8 miles run
Wednesday:   15 miles run
Thursday:    rest
Friday:      4 miles run
Saturday:    10 miles run
*weekly mileage 66 miles*

**Week 24.**
Sunday:      15 miles run
Monday:      6 miles run
Tuesday:     10 miles run
Wednesday:   18 miles run
Thursday:    8 miles run

Friday:      rest
Saturday:    15 miles run
*weekly mileage 72 miles*

**Week 25.**
Sunday:      10 miles run
Monday:      8 miles run
Tuesday:     6 miles at a good
             pace
Wednesday:   15 miles run
Thursday:    8 miles run
Friday:      4 miles run
Saturday:    12 miles run
*weekly mileage 63 miles*

**Week 26.**
Sunday:      8 miles run
Monday:      6 miles run
Tuesday:     6 miles run
Wednesday:   rest
Thursday:    4 miles jog
Friday:      rest
Saturday:    *Marathon race*

## Notes on the schedule:

**1.** The jog/walk sessions are mainly jogging but the walking is for when the runner finds breathing becomes too quick or feels just too much tiredness in the legs.
**2.** The walk when done as part of the schedule should be done with an easy long stride, not back from the shops pulling a shopping trolley. It could however be accomplished by walking to pick the children up from school instead of taking the car or by getting off the bus or train one stop early when coming home from work.
**3.** The races are included so that the novice to road running will find out what is involved in racing over the road.
**4.** Should the marathon you have selected for your first one be on a Sunday the final week's training would be adjusted as follows:

SUNDAY      8 miles run
MONDAY      6 miles run
TUESDAY     rest

WEDNESDAY 6 miles run
THURSDAY   rest
FRIDAY     4 miles jog
SATURDAY   rest
SUNDAY     Marathon race

Even if you do not have immediate ambitions for the marathon this schedule will get you started into regular exercise and you can progress to whatever level satisfies you. Your aim could be to run in short road races up to 10 kilometres or to be a regular competitor in 10 mile road races. Should you be going up to the marathon distance there are a number of other factors apart from training for you to take into consideration.

One of the problems the long distance runner must face is the production of heat through continuous exercise for a long period. The body has a natural cooling system which works by increasing the blood flow in the body to try and maintain an even temperature throughout the body and also sweating to cool the body surface. The cooling comes about as the sweat evaporates. In humid conditions sweat cannot evaporate, therefore cooling does not take place as it would in dry conditions. While temperature may be kept down by sweating, the loss of water creates another problem, if allowed to continue without any precaution then the body would dehydrate. It is therefore essential that the long-distance runner pays attention to the intake of water not just in the long distance races but also in training. Joyce has found that the best way for her to drink while running is by using small plastic bottles sold in chemists empty for filling with hair spray or the like. These bottles have a small hole in the screw-on top. By squeezing the bottle, the liquid in the bottle is squirted into your mouth. Joyce finds this a better way to drink than from a bottle with an open top because then drinks are gulped down and unless the bottle is kept still the drink will slop out. The bottle is also small enough so that you can run with it in your hand without losing any drink. Fill it with water, fruit juice or electrolyte drink, whatever you prefer. Joyce prefers a diluted lemon/lime barley water drink. Beware of too much or too rich a glucose mix as this has been known to cause stomach trouble. In mass marathons individual drinks are not possible and cardboard cups are available, generally half filled, at refreshment stations. If you squeeze the top of the cup you stop the liquid coming out of the cup and you make a funnel of sorts to pour the drink into your mouth without splashing it over the rest of your face and down your chest.

Joyce has lost up to 6 pounds in weight during a marathon and most of that loss is water and this is in spite of drinking during the race. If Joyce hadn't taken in liquid the loss could have been much greater but quite possibly she would have collapsed, dehydrated. Before Joyce ran her first marathon she practised drinking while running. If you cannot find a friend to assist you on a training run by cycling with you and passing you a drink when it is needed, run circuits past your house on your long runs, and

*Taking drinks during a marathon.*

have the drinks outside ready for you. One person we knew used to drive out over the course he was going to run and hide his bottles of drink in bushes around the course then when he ran he took the drinks as he passed the different spots where he had hidden them. The rules in Britain for taking refreshment in a race only allow drinks to be taken in races over 10 miles. In marathons drinks may be provided at every 5 kilometres, and in between drink points sponging points can be provided.

Hot weather is one of the distance runner's greatest enemies and apart from drinking while running to combat the effects of the sun, wear pale-coloured or white clothing. Light colours reflect the heat while dark colours attract the heat. Marathon runners therefore need to wear light coloured vests to reflect heat away from the body and the vest should also be loose fitting to enable air to reach the skin and speed up the evaporation of sweat, thereby allowing some cooling to take place. String or mesh vests, of course allow more air to reach the body and while they may not look great, they may enable you to feel great. While hot weather creates a problem for the marathon runner because of the need to dissipate body heat, in cold weather you need to ensure the body temperature does not drop below normal and increased clothing will generally have this effect. In the winter Joyce has always raced in a long-sleeved vest and most training sessions are done in a track suit.

Having decided what to wear for your marathon race you will no doubt, be wondering whether you should follow a special marathon diet. The marathon diet in general follows a plan like this:

| DAY 1 | protein and fat diet | normal training |
| DAY 2 | protein and fat diet | normal training |
| DAY 3 | protein and fat diet | normal training |
| DAY 4 | carbohydrate diet | easy or no training |
| DAY 5 | carbohydrate diet | easy or no training |
| DAY 6 | carbohydrate diet | rest |
| DAY 7 | race Day. | |

During the first three days of the diet the athlete eats

*Joyce wears a long-sleeved top during a marathon run on a cool day. Joyce shares her drink with a Norwegian fellow competitor; it is against the rules, but promotes international friendship.*

mainly meat and salads, but no bread, potatoes etc. During the three days prior to the race the athlete goes to town on the pasta, cakes, bread, potatoes etc. The body having been fooled in the first three days into thinking there is a carbohydrate shortage, stocks up the larder when carbohydrate becomes available in the next three days, and therefore has plenty of this energy-giving food to see the athlete through any continuous exercise that will take longer than two hours. This diet doesn't work for everyone. Some athletes have found that just taking the carbohydrate loading without the protein diet helps them. Certainly, tests carried out by physiologists have indicated a sound basis for this. What is also apparent is that if this type of dieting is done too often the body compensates and the extra carbohydrate loses its effect. Joyce has only tried the diet a couple of times. Prior to her two fastest times in the 1981 and 1982 London Marathons she just had a good carbohydrate based meal the night before the race, and for breakfast toast with honey. One advantage of eating plenty of carbohydrates is that carbohydrates have a great affinity with water and the body stores more water which means, of course, it has more to call upon during the exercise of distance running.

During the road race, no matter whether the distance is five miles or a marathon, pacing yourself is important. In the race the mile points should be signposted, if not it is worth trying to find out where they are, you may be able to drive the course and measure them roughly on the car mileometer. Joyce wears a black plastic watch that doubles as a stop-watch as well as a time of day watch. By starting the stop-watch when the gun goes she is able to check her time at any point on the course. She, as would most other runners, would be aiming for a certain time which should always be a realistic aim. Then, after working out the pace for that time she will have some indication at the mile markers en route of how she is running. Some athletes write their pace times on the back of their hand or arm so they don't forget. If you do this use waterproof ink otherwise the sweat from your arm will wash it off! If you don't fancy walking around with figures on your arm for the next few days you can write them on a wrist band, on a handkerchief or on a piece of plaster stuck on your watch strap. The marathon pace chart in Appendix 3 will give you a guide as to what is required for level pace running. You should practise some pace judgement during your training runs. Measure out your various courses from where you train. They need not be absolutely accurate so you can do a rough measure on an Ordnance Survey map which will give you a useful indication.

On one of Joyce's courses which she uses for her long runs she comes to some cross roads in 51 minutes, should she be slower she knows she must either pick the pace up or expect a slower final time. If it is faster then she should try and maintain the same pace, but stay relaxed. If you deliberately slow down, you will probably find you will slow too much. Should you be running too fast for the pace aimed at, think of relaxing rather than slowing; sometimes there is a reason for the faster pace, you could have been running slightly downhill or the wind could have been with you. By knowing your usual time on certain parts of your training courses, you can vary your training by running the first part slow and the second half fast, or vice-versa. That watch on your wrist is going to be a valuable running aid.

When you come across the line after your marathon there will be feeling of relief and you will be wondering what your time was and your position in the race. The same applies to all road races. Your watch will provide you with your time for the race – assuming you remembered to stop it when you crossed the line! Having been running over 26 miles, to suddenly stop causes all sorts of aches, pains and stiffness to occur. Try and keep walking around, have a drink, put a track-suit top over your shoulders. When you feel recovered in your breathing put your track suit bottoms on and try to keep moving until you feel 'cooled down', then take a shower or bath.

After a marathon Joyce likes to have a long hot bath, deep enough to completely cover the legs. The warm water stimulates the circulation in the legs and helps the disbursement of the lactic acid from the muscles which is what stiffens you up. Some easy toe touching in the bath helps stretch those muscles at the back of the legs. The bath may be taken some hours after the finish but it certainly relaxes you. The next day a 2- or 3-mile run may feel awkward, but it is the best way to get your body back to normal, then the following day a 5- or 6-mile run. For the rest of the week distances of runs would range between 5 to 8 miles.

*Joyce surrounded by male runners in the 1982 London marathon.*

After your first marathon you may well be thinking of the next one. The following 12-week schedule is provided for those who are already training regularly and are thinking of running a marathon competitively, rather than just completing the distance.

# A 12-WEEK BUILD UP TO THE MARATHON

**Week 1.**
Sunday:       15 miles run,
              nice and easy
Monday:       8 miles run
Tuesday:      10 miles run with
              some strides to
              stretch the legs
Wednesday: 12 miles run easy
Thursday:  6 miles run
Friday:    rest
Saturday:  12 miles run
*weekly mileage 63 miles*

**Week 2.**
Sunday:       10 miles run
Monday:       8 miles run
Tuesday:      15 × 400 metres with
              200 metres jog
              recovery on the track
              including warm up,
              minimum total
              distance 6 miles
Wednesday: 15 miles run easy
Thursday:  8 miles run
Friday:    5 miles easy
Saturday:  15 miles run
*weekly mileage 68 miles*

**Week 3.**
Sunday:       15 miles run
Monday:       5 miles run
              fairly hard
Tuesday:      on the track 6 × 800
              metres with
              400-metres jog
              recovery including
              warming up,
              total distance
              6 miles running
Wednesday: 18 miles run easy
Thursday:  6 miles run
Friday:    5 miles run easy
Saturday:  12 miles run
*weekly mileage 67 miles*

**Week 4.**
Sunday:       18 miles run easy
Monday:       5 miles run
Tuesday:      10 miles run with
              some strides or
              fast runs varying
              from 200 metres
              to 600 metres.
Wednesday: 12 miles run
Thursday:  8 miles run
Friday:    rest
Saturday:  8 miles in morning,
           5 miles in
           afternoon or evening
*weekly mileage 66 miles*

**Week 5.**
Sunday:       18 miles run
Monday:       8 miles run
Tuesday:      4 × 1200 metres on
              the track with 400
              metres jog recovery
              total distance
              including warm up
              6 miles minimum
Wednesday: 15 miles run
Thursday:  8 miles run
Friday:    5 miles run easy
Saturday:  10 miles run
*weekly mileage 70 miles*

**Week 6.**
Sunday:       20 miles run
Monday:       12 miles run
Tuesday:      6 miles fast
Wednesday: 12 miles run easy
Thursday:  4 × 1 mile with 5
           minutes rest
           recovery
Friday:    rest
Saturday:  *10 miles road race*
           or 12 miles
           training run
*weekly mileage 68 miles*

**Week 7.**

| | |
|---|---|
| Sunday: | 20 miles run |
| Monday: | 8 miles run |
| Tuesday: | 10 miles run with strides as previously |
| Wednesday: | 15 miles run |
| Thursday: | 8 miles run |
| Friday: | 5 miles easy run |
| Saturday: | morning 18 miles, afternoon or evening 3 miles fast run |

*weekly mileage 87 miles*

**Week 8.**

| | |
|---|---|
| Sunday: | 10 miles run |
| Monday: | 8 miles run |
| Tuesday: | 6 miles fast run |
| Wednesday: | 18 miles run |
| Thursday: | 8 miles run |
| Friday: | 5 miles easy run |
| Saturday: | 12 miles run |

*weekly mileage 67 miles*

**Week 9.**

| | |
|---|---|
| Sunday: | 22 miles easy run |
| Monday: | 5 miles run |
| Tuesday: | 10 miles run with strides as before |
| Wednesday: | 15 miles run |
| Thursday: | 6 miles run |
| Friday: | 5 miles run |
| Saturday: | morning 15 miles, afternoon or evening 5 miles run |

*weekly mileage 73 miles*

**Week 10.**

| | |
|---|---|
| Sunday: | 20 miles run |
| Monday: | 5 miles easy run |
| Tuesday: | 8 miles run |
| Wednesday: | 18 miles run |
| Thursday: | 6 miles run |
| Friday: | rest |
| Saturday: | 20 miles run |

*weekly mileage 77 miles*

**Week 11.**

| | |
|---|---|
| Sunday: | 15 miles run |
| Monday: | 8 miles run |
| Tuesday: | 10 miles run with strides as before |
| Wednesday: | 15 miles run |
| Thursday: | 8 miles run |
| Friday: | rest |
| Saturday: | 12 miles run |

*weekly mileage 68 miles*

**Week 12.**

| | |
|---|---|
| Sunday: | 10 miles run |
| Monday: | rest |
| Tuesday: | 6 miles run |
| Wednesday: | easy 4 miles jog |
| Thursday: | rest |
| Friday: | easy 4 miles jog |
| Saturday: | *marathon race* |

*(If the race is on Sunday, then Saturday would be a rest day)*

NOTES: The long runs of 18 miles and above would be run at an easy pace. The track sessions such as 15 × 400 metres could be done on the road or in the park if a track is not available. They must be preceded by a warm up and concluded with a jog to ease and cool the body down.

The main problem in completing a faster marathon is maintaining the pace for the whole of the 26 miles, 385 yards. You can find out what it is like to run faster by competing in the road races over shorter distances than a marathon, such as 10 miles, half-marathon and 25 kilometres or 15 miles. But to combat the tiredness that comes at the end of the marathon that experience must be simulated in training perhaps by trying to run that bit faster over the last few miles of a 15-mile training run. That is not to say every training run is a question of pushing yourself to exhaustion. If you did that you would soon find yourself struggling to walk to the station let alone go out running in the evening. One or perhaps two hard runs a week in training are sufficient. Don't forget after training and a shower you should be looking forward to the next training session. Don't push yourself to the extent of resenting your training. Running is about enjoyment.

There has been a bias here on marathon running but many runners receive much satisfaction in competing in 10-mile races or races around that distance. 10-mile races have their own challenge to break the hour, 70-minute or

*The popularity of marathon running can be seen by the number of spectators who turned out to watch the start and finish of the Osaka ladies' marathon.*

90-minute barrier. They can of course, be run more often than marathon races as they are less stressful. A typical week's training for the 10-mile racing might be as follows:

| | |
|---|---|
| SUNDAY | 12 miles steady run |
| MONDAY | 6 miles fartlek |
| TUESDAY | track session perhaps 5 × 800 metres |
| WEDNESDAY | 8 miles steady run |
| THURSDAY | 5 miles fast road run |
| FRIDAY | 5 miles easy or rest |
| SATURDAY | cross-country club race or |
| | 6 miles training run |

The value of 10-mile races for the marathoner is that they help build up speed for marathon races. After all if you cannot run a good 10-miler you are unlikely to run a good marathon.

# The day of the race

The day of the race – you didn't sleep well the night before, one of your muscles feels stiff, there is a pain in one of your ankles, and to cap it all everyone in the household is doing things wrong, don't they realize you are racing today! Your nerves will certainly play you up before an important race. You could well be wondering why you took up running. After the race it is all so different, the feeling of having accomplished what you set out to do, a sense of achievement, the pleasure of finishing the race in a good time. The person who annoyed you in the dressing room because he or she wouldn't stop talking is now a pleasant conversationalist, everyone chats happily about the race, their performance, your performance. There is an air of camaraderie in the dressing rooms and in the tea room after everyone has finished.

The day of the race, the day the adrenalin really flows. You discover your strengths and your weaknesses as well as those of others. It is the day when you will find out if all those training hours have been sufficient. It will be a day to be remembered.

Preparing for the race means planning your training but you also need to consider carefully just what might be involved. It may seem a silly thing to say, but having selected the race you are going to run in, don't forget to enter it. If the race is abroad you will need permission from

*The faces show how nervous tension builds up prior to the start of the race but all the athletes keep warm.*

your sport's governing body. It has been known for athletes to do everything right in preparing for a race but then forget the essentials of getting into the race.

Fortunately we in Britain live in a fairly temperate climate and therefore do not have to worry too much about racing in different extremes of temperature. We do have our odd hot day and should you find the conditions are warm then make sure you take all the necessary precautions – light coloured and loose clothing, drink before you race and if you are competing in a marathon

117

take drinks at every refreshment point. If you wait until you feel thirsty or dry then you have left it too late. Take advantage of the wet sponges that are offered in marathons. Don't just sponge your face, that will refresh you but if you sponge your arms and legs you will be putting cool water on the body which helps lower body temperature and also when that water evaporates there is an additional cooling effect. It is worth making sure that you do sponge the legs and do not just squeeze the water out of the sponge onto the legs. If you do the latter there is a good chance that the water will soak your shoes and that can cause your feet to move about more and bring on blisters. As a final precaution, don't go into a race when the weather conditions are bad for running thinking you are going to run a personal best. You can run to beat other runners but if you try to beat the weather you could be a bad second best.

One other condition which requires you to be careful and watch the speed at which you are running is at altitude.

*Sponging down in the marathon to keep cool.*

The higher you go the less dense the air, hence there is less oxygen available for the body which will affect the amount of exercise that can be done in comfort. At high altitude the air is drier, therefore evaporation from the body is greater, so liquid consumption needs to be increased. To compete successfully at altitude needs a good period of acclimatisation.

If you are in a position to compete abroad, it is not just the weather and altitude of the area in which you are competing that has to be allowed for. You must remember that the difference in time must be taken into account. In normal day to day living your body becomes used to the usual pattern your life follows (diurnal variation) such as regular times for eating, going to bed and getting up. Just as the body becomes accustomed to the normal daily routine it adjusts to training at certain times. Many athletes who train after work and race perhaps Saturday afternoons have complained they didn't feel right when racing one morning. This is the effect of the body not being used to exercising at that time. Before a major race Joyce will find out the time of the race and train at that time

*A major marathon needs adjustment to your normal routine.*

some weeks beforehand so that she changes her body pattern for the race. This has applied to major races she has competed in on the track, cross-country and road.

Similarly it's worth finding out what routine is followed at the big races you are competing in. It could be completely different to the routine you follow in a training session. Generally an athlete turns up for training, warms up, does some exercises and then goes straight into the major part of the session. Championships don't follow that pattern. At an Olympic Games or major athletic championship after warming up, the athletes are called to an assembly area and have their spikes, numbers and clothing checked and it could be up to 20 minutes from the end of the warm up to the time the athlete toes the line at the start. It is therefore essential the athlete finds a way to keep the body warm during this waiting period and more importantly becomes used to this routine. Joyce would arrange her training sessions prior to these big competitions to try out ways of keeping warm in a confined space and to let her body become accustomed to a gap in activity between warming up and competition. In a marathon this problem is not so bad as very little warm up is needed but there are the problems of registration, getting to your right position on the start and ensuring your track suit is being looked after while you are competing.

Having found out everything you need to know before the day of the race so that you can plan accordingly, pack your bag with care. You will probably have packed your bag for training and other races many times but the way even experienced athletes have arrived at a venue without shorts, shoes or with two left ones, towels or any item that is vital is amazing. Mentally dress yourself as you pack your bag: start from the bottom with shoes, socks, shorts, underwear, vests (different types to cater for weather conditions) track suit, rain or wet suit and so on. Don't forget toilet bag and towel, Vaseline for toes and any area of the body which might rub or be rubbed, talcum powder, spare shoe laces, spare screw-in spikes and spike spanner if you are going to a track race, safety pins – eight at least and plastic bags, one to put wet shoes in, another for your number in case it rains and one additional as a spare for emergency. The items suggested above serve as a basis for any runner's race-day needs but you will discover your own requirements and build up your own list. Marathon runners should remember they need drink containers.

Having packed your bag before leaving home, remember to take your travel directions with you. You don't want to spend half an hour wandering around a town asking where the race meeting is taking place.

## CROSS-COUNTRY RACES

Arrive early, so allowing yourself plenty of time to have a look at the course. Some runners like to change into their running gear early to allow their body to become accustomed to it, others change late, there are no advantages in either so it is just a question of what you prefer. Some walk the course, others jog the course as part of the warm up. If you do not like to spend too much time jogging or walking around the course (if it's a one-loop 5-mile course you wouldn't want to run round it) look at the start and the finish and find a few points on the course from which you can observe most of the route the race will follow. For a major race Joyce and I will walk the course together perhaps with some of the other members of Joyce's team. At the start we check the length of the starting straight (the distance from the starting line to the first bend) and whether the field goes left or right after the initial straight. If you start on the right and the first bend is to the right you can find yourself trapped behind the athletes from the left who will swing across the other competitors. What is the ground surface like? If it is even you can run concentrating on position, if it is rough you will have to watch where you are putting your feet. On the course we watch for narrow openings – getting caught behind a group trying to squeeze through would mean the race leader would be able to break-away. If there are hills, know where they are situated in the race, the third quarter of a race is the most tiring part and often the part where races are won and lost. Then on cross-country courses look for ditches or streams that may have to be jumped and have a couple of practice jumps to find the best angle of approach and the safest landing spot. Don't forget if there are other races before yours which have to go over the same spot it could look completely different when you come to it in the race. If there are hurdles or obstacles on the course try them out and make sure you can negotiate them swiftly and safely. In the final stretch into the finish look to see how far away from the finish line you can start your last effort. If it is an uphill finish you may leave it fairly late in the race, should it be a downhill finish you could start pushing the pace faster much earlier. Once you have seen the course try and imagine how your rivals are going to run, then work out your own race plan.

## ROAD RACES

There are many similarities to the way you look at the course for cross-country and road races. Obviously you do not need to pay so much attention to the road surface but do watch out for cobble stones, pot holes,

*Check the course for type of surface and camber, this level cycle-way provides no problems, but athletes should know what lies ahead and be prepared for it.*

*All numbers should be pinned on securely!*

drains, the camber of the road and so on. If you are running in a group you cannot always see immediately what lies ahead and many an ankle has been turned in a pot hole because of that. Constantly running on a camber can cause a strain on the legs – often the camber is less if you run closer to the kerb. Sometimes the route a road race will follow is a public footpath, these can be narrow so it is worth checking them out before the race. If you are catching a group of runners it may be worth putting an extra effort in to get past them before a footpath, otherwise you may be forced to run behind them for the whole length of the footpath thereby losing time. Often a plea to let you pass will work and slower runners will make way for you. Jogging or walking a road race course is often impossible because of its length, so a car ride round may be the only way to view it. Otherwise a map of the course should be available and you can check over the map for footpaths, major or minor roads so that you have an idea of where you are running.

Having checked the course for either cross-country or road races find out where the nearest toilets are. It is

*After the race keep warm and take fluid.*

*Warm down as soon as you have recovered from the race or training session.*

surprising how the anxiety caused by the approaching start time of a race can agitate you and bring on an urgent need to find a lavatory. We know of one competitor who was caught short like this before her first marathon and started the race 5 minutes late as a result!

Obtain your race number either from the organisers or your team manager and pin it on securely and comfortably, you don't want to have to worry about that during a race. Most race numbers are cardboard so Joyce goes prepared with a clear plastic bag in her holdall and if rain threatens she puts the number in the plastic bag before pinning it on. In a long road race rain can disintegrate a number quite easily and it can cause chaos if judges cannot record your number.

During the hours before a race try and remain relaxed and calm. For some people that means keeping busy so that their mind is not on the race. If you have to keep busy don't start spring cleaning on the morning of the race – energy expenditure needs to be kept to a minimum. Others are happy quietly reading a book or a magazine.

After the race you need to cool down or warm down and some easy jogging in your track suit will slowly bring your muscles, heart beat, breathing and blood flow back to normal and in doing so you will aid the body in getting rid of the waste products such as lactic acid and carbon-dioxide. Instead of feeling stiff the next day you will be ready for your next training session, which doesn't have to be a hard run, it could be an easy jog or even a swim. If you really feel tired then have a day off. Don't feel guilty about having a rest, it could be just what you need to let the body recover after a tough race or training session.

# Ladies only

Today the woman in sport is very much socially accepted, no longer the odd one out as she used to be not so many years ago. However, while the female athlete has been making rapid advances in the sport, and there has been much talk about the possibility of women catching up with the speed of men and in some events being their equal, it must be recognized that there are undisputable physiological differences between men and women.

Throughout the world the female has been cast in a certain role and that role has changed as time has gone by. It has been generally accepted in the Western world that the female, because she is the bearer of the children, leads a more domestic life. She has been the minder of the children, the house cleaner, the cook, whereas with the traditional male role of provider has gone a certain amount of leisure time that could be spent playing sport, amongst other things. Times have changed and now leisure time has increased both for men and women.

Because of woman's child-bearing role, she is designed differently to man in many areas not always readily apparent. Women are on average both shorter and lighter than men and also the fat distribution between the sexes is not the same. Women tend to have fatty tissue around the hips and thigh region which will lower the centre of gravity of the female compared to the male, which in turn

*Joyce out jogging with Lisa while expecting Lia.*

affects the mechanical performance in running and other sports. On average the woman has about 30% of her total weight composed of fatty tissue compared to a man's 20%. When you compare muscle tissue, the female has about 36% of her total weight composed of muscle whereas the man has about 40% of his total weight. Man has 20% of his weight in bone to the woman's 15%, man has more blood – 8% to 7%, his lungs average 1·35 kilogrammes to her 1·05 kilogrammes. In the blood is a substance called haemoglobin which enables oxygen to be carried around the body. A man on average has 15·8 grammes of haemoglobin per 100 millilitres of blood to the woman's 13·7 grammes per 100 millilitres of blood. Generally oxygen uptake, an essential ingredient in human exercise, when related to body weight, is 15 to 20% lower in post-pubertal women compared to men.

The figures I have given above put the female at a functional disadvantage to the male and for this reason alone there is no need to compare male and female performance. However, in a competitive world, when competitions are governed by the measurement of one person's performance compared to another, it is inevitable that there will be comparison of male and female. It is no good making a comparison between husband and wife or girlfriend and boyfriend as each person will have different natural attributes. There was an article recently in an American magazine about the increased divorce rate between couples where both partners were runners but it mistakenly blamed running for being the cause.

Coming back to real comparisons, competitions must match like with like and the world records set out on p. 130 show that men and women are unevenly matched in athletics.

## RECORDS AS AT 31ST AUGUST 1982

It can be seen from the percentage difference between the male and the female world records that there is an approximate 10% difference between the two sexes. One factor that must be carefully noted is that over the years women's records have tumbled quite regularly and rapidly especially in those events in which women have not competed until recently such as the marathon. This tremendous advance when compared to the advancement of the men's records does not mean that the women are catching the men up, as has been suggested in some quarters. This performance chart illustrates the comparative speed achievements of men and women. The following graph shows the progress of the men's and women's world marathon best performances.

| | Men | Women | Percentage difference in performance |
|---|---|---|---|
| 100 metres | 9·95 | 10·88 | 91·45 |
| 200 metres | 19·83 | 21·71 | 91·34 |
| 400 metres | 43·86 | 48·60 | 90·25 |
| 800 metres | 1:41·73 | 1:53·43 | 89·69 |
| 1500 metres | 3:31·36 | 3:52·47 | 90·91 |
| 1 mile | 3:47·33 | 4:18·08 | 88·09 |
| 3000 metres | 7:32·01 | 8:26·08 | 89·21 |
| 5000 metres | 13:00·42 | 15:08·26 | 85·93 |
| 10,000 metres | 27:22·05 | 31:35·03 | 86·66 |
| Marathon | 2hrs 08:13 | 2 hrs 25:29 | 88·13 |

Although the women have quickly come closer to the men their graph line will even out to run parallel with the men. The reason for their rapid advancement is only due to more women taking part in the event. In Britain, it wasn't until 1978 that there was a marathon championship for women.

The majority of road races today are combined, with men and women running together. Going on the figures mentioned above, a top-class woman could find herself finishing a race with more men behind her than in front. Running in with men has an advantage for the woman – there are more people to run with which can act as a spur to continually move up to the competitor in front. This is easier to do if your rival is only a few yards in front rather than hundreds of yards. In general most runners help each other in races and most men will try and help the lady runner to a better time – really we have a legalised form of

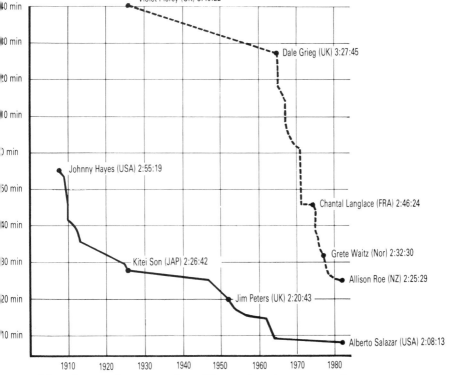

*Marathon performance chart illustrating the comparative speed achievements of men and women. More detail is given in the lists on pages 135–136.*

pacing in mixed races. Female-only races are completely different to mixed races. They are more tactical, and can mean running by yourself which involves setting your own pace but has the advantage of knowing exactly how you are placed in relation to your fellow competitors. Sometimes in mixed races if you are in with a bunch of men there could be a woman who you want to beat fairly close to you without you knowing it. Basically a women's only race provides fairer competition but a mixed race will probably provide better times.

The one time in a woman's running career when her times do not improve is during pregnancy. The effects and

131

enjoyment of running during pregnancy vary from woman to woman. We have known women who have continued running, or rather jogging, right up to the time of the birth whereas others have stopped just after learning of the pregnancy. Fortunately in most countries doctors monitor women during pregnancy very well with monthly check ups at least and consequently the doctor can advise on what you should be doing. Joyce carried on training through both her pregnancies and in the second pregnancy competed in the first two months. As long as you err on the side of caution it can be quite safe to go on running. Obviously you no longer consider racing hard or in important races because of the stress factors involved and by cutting out such racing there is no longer a need to think of training for a specific event, therefore training

*Joyce running in with a group of men during the London marathon.*

*Joyce was two months pregnant when competing in the City of London 3 miles race in 1979.*

takes on a new meaning. Training is now aimed at maintaining a level of personal fitness, it keeps the weight in check which can so easily go up when running stops. It also helps the return to fitness after the birth.

You may well find it impossible to rush back to racing fitness soon after the birth and you don't need to do so. First of all wait until after the post-natal check-up before doing anything, although post-natal exercises will help tighten the slack abdominal muscles and walking with the pram is another form of exercise that will help the new mother become fitter. After the check-up you will know that there are no problems or hitches that will stop you getting back into running. You will, of course, have junior to look after and the baby will be very demanding of your time. If you are going to breast feed the baby for as long as possible then you should think of an even slower return to racing fitness. The return to running fitness is similar to the experience of starting to run, when you first start except that if you did train before the birth you can speed up the process. First of all, try running a couple of times a week for three or four weeks depending on how you feel.

133

The distance may only be a mile, or even less on the first outing, but on each subsequent session you could well find that the distance can be increased by stages until by the third or fourth week you are running four miles in one session. From then on increase the number of sessions and on one particular session in each week use it as a build up for distance running if that is what you are particularly aiming for. Otherwise your aim is to regain your normal fitness, getting rid of the extra weight that is carried after the birth until you are back to what is your normal weight, and of course plenty of exercises to tone up and stretch those muscles in the legs.

It has often been found that women who come back into athletics after having a baby run even better than before. Certainly Joyce has continued to improve after each of her pregnancies. It is believed that one of the reasons for this is that during the pregnancy the body increases the production of a hormone, relaxin, which brings greater suppleness to the woman. Its purpose is to assist in making the birth that much easier. The hormone does not disappear after the birth and the woman is left with this natural hormone which gives her a greater range of movement and therefore in essence makes her a better athlete.

Menstruation pains can be a problem for some women but you often find that with the increase in fitness that running brings painful periods are no longer a real worry. There is almost certainly no reason to stop running during menstruation. From data available, it is known that a number of female athletes have won Olympic gold medals during menstruation. However, should the monthly period be an inconvenience then the training programme can be adjusted so that a monthly schedule would follow three weeks' hard and intensive training by one week easy training. For example a marathon runner of international standard may follow the schedule below:

**week one**    80 miles total during the week
**week two**    90 miles total during the week
**week three** 80 miles total during the week
**week four**  50 miles total during the week

However some women have found that when they start hard training their periods stop, which is known as amenorrhoea. This has happened to some of the world's top female distance runners and apart from stopping any monthly disruption to training is an advantage in that the blood can carry more oxygen to muscles which is a distinct aid to training and racing.

In conclusion it must be appreciated that there are differences between male and female athletes and while women are unable to expect the same results as men, there is no reason why women should not compete and enjoy all forms of sport.

# WORLD MARATHON RECORDS OVER THE YEARS

**Men**

| | | | |
|---|---|---|---|
| 2:55:19 | Johnny Hayes | USA | 24.7.1908 |
| 2:52:46 | Robert Fowler | USA | 1.1.1909 |
| 2:46:53 | James Clark | USA | 12.2.1909 |
| 2:46:05 | Albert Raines | USA | 8.5.1909 |
| 2:42:31 | Fred Barrett | UK | 25.5.1909 |
| 2:38:17 | Harry Green | UK | 12.5.1913 |
| 2:36:07 | Alexis Ahlgren | SWE | 31.5.1913 |
| 2:32:36 | Hannes Kolehmainen | FIN | 22.8.1920 |
| 2:29:02 | Al Michelson | USA | 12.10.1925 |
| 2:27:49 | Fusashige Suzuki | JAP | 31.3.1935 |
| 2:26:44 | Yasuo Ikenaka | JAP | 4.4.1935 |
| 2:26:42 | Kitei Son | JAP | 23.11.1935 |
| 2:25:39 | Yun Bok Suh | KOR | 19.4.1947 |
| 2:20:43 | Jim Peters | UK | 11.6.1952 |
| 2:18:41 | Jim Peters | UK | 13.6.1953 |
| 2:18:35 | Jim Peters | UK | 4.10.1953 |
| 2:17:40 | Jim Peters | UK | 26.6.1954 |
| 2:15:17 | Sergey Popov | USSR | 24.8.1958 |
| 2:15:17 | Abebe Bikila | ETH | 10.9.1960 |
| 2:15:16 | Toru Terasawa | JAP | 17.2.1963 |
| 2:14:28 | Buddy Edelen | USA | 15.6.1963 |
| 2:13:55 | Basil Heatley | UK | 13.6.1964 |
| 2:12:12 | Abebe Bikila | ETH | 21.10.1964 |
| 2:12:00 | Morio Shigematsu | JAP | 12.6.1965 |
| 2:09:37 | Derek Clayton | AUS | 3.12.1967 |
| 2:08:34 | Derek Clayton | AUS | 30.5.1969 |
| 2:08:13 | Alberto Salazar | USA | 25.10.1981 |

## Women

| | | | |
|---|---|---|---|
| 3:40:22 | Violet Piercy | UK | 3.10.1926 |
| 3:27:45 | Dale Grieg | UK | 23.5.1964 |
| 3:19:33 | Millie Sampson | NZ | 21.7.1964 |
| 3:15:22 | Maureen Wilton | CAN | 6.5.1967 |
| 3:07:26 | Anni Pede-Erdkamp | GER | 16.9.1967 |
| 3:02:53 | Caroline Walker | USA | 28.2.1970 |
| 3:01:42 | Beth Bonner | USA | 9.5.1971 |
| 2:46:30 | Adrienne Beames | AUS | 31.8.1971 |
| 2:46:24 | Chantal Langlace | FRA | 27.10.1974 |
| 2:43:55 | Jackie Hansen | USA | 1.12.1974 |
| 2:42:24 | Liane Winter | GER | 21.4.1975 |
| 2:40:16 | Christa Vahlensieck | GER | 3.5.1975 |
| 2:38:19 | Jackie Hansen | USA | 12.10.1975 |
| 2:35:16 | Chantal Langlace | FRA | 1.5.1977 |
| 2:34:48 | Christa Vahlensieck | GER | 10.9.1977 |
| 2:32:30 | Grete Waitz | NOR | 22.10.1978 |
| 2:27:33 | Grete Waitz | NOR | 21.10.1979 |
| 2:25:42 | Grete Waitz | NOR | 26.10.1980 |
| 2:25:29 | Allison Roe | NZ | 25.10.1981 |

# You are never too old

It has been said that after puberty man is naturally a lazy animal and the cells in his body begin to degenerate. Degeneration is the start of ageing. Exercise keeps cells active and stops degeneration, exercise therefore stops ageing. The conclusions to be drawn from this are obvious. Thankfully today it is becoming more and more acceptable for all ages to take part in sport just as it is now acceptable to society for women to take part in sport. In the not too distant past veteran athletes would have had people coming up to them saying, "you shouldn't be doing that at your age". There has always been a readiness to write someone off because of their age. Campaigns such as 'Sport for All' have made many of us aware that sport is not only for teenagers and those in their twenties. Regrettably the message hasn't reached everybody yet.

In 1975 Joyce, who was then 37, twisted her ankle while out training and it turned out to be an injury that would not get better. Joyce received physiotherapy and the ankle was even put in plaster for a month to reduce movement in the hope that complete immobility of the ankle would cure it. But it did not and the doctor informed her that she had osteo-arthritis and would have to 'call it a day', age had caught up with her and you can't expect to keep going for ever. The doctor agreed to Joyce taking a second opinion, as we could not believe she could be written off six months

*Joyce, although she has been classified as a veteran for years, keeps on improving.*

after being placed in the European Athletic Championships. Fortunately for Joyce, the second doctor diagnosed a strained tendon and treated that successfully and by the end of the 1975 summer season she was back in the British athletic team. Since that injury Joyce has, of course, continued in athletics. In fact since that injury Joyce had our second daughter in 1976 and in 1978 broke a bone in her foot while competing for Great Britain against France in a track 3000-metre race. On both occasions she could have retired, but sport is something to be enjoyed and is a hobby and you don't give up something you enjoy just because of age. Joyce has therefore continued competing in athletics and has continued to improve and it is particularly pleasing to us to hear of many veterans who continue to improve their personal athletic records. In 1979 Joyce was selected by *The Observer* as their "Mum" Sports Personality of the Year for her performances in the marathon and David Hunn of *The Observer* wrote "that Joyce has opened two significant doors: one was marked, 'Women must not run through here' and the other 'Over-forties keep out'." These words not only demonstrated what Joyce had achieved but highlighted what should be accepted by everyone.

Veterans' athletics is now accepted throughout the world with World, Continent and National Championships, and most road races offer 'vets prizes'. The age groupings are arranged in 5-year stages, for women 35 to 40, 40 to 45, 45 to 50, etc., and for men 40 to 45, 45 to 50, etc. Thus competition is provided between those in the same age groups just as is done at the other end of the age scale with girls being under 13, juniors under 15 and intermediates under 17 on the ladies' side, and with colts of under 13, boys under 15, youths under 17 and juniors under 20. In veterans' athletics we have athletes looking forward to their next birthday when it takes them up into the next age grouping. Who would have thought people would want to be older!

While most of us would like to be at a physical peak forever, age does bring about a gradual deterioration in physical performance. Statistics taken on numbers of people of various ages have shown that a person reaches maximum muscular strength between the ages of 20 and 30, after which there is a gradual decline in strength. 65-year-olds can expect to be approximately 65% below their maximum level of strength. A similar story is found from measurements taken of oxygen uptake levels which demonstrates aerobic power. This is at a peak around the ages of 18 to 20 and then gradually decreases so that when you are 65 it will be about 70% of the level it was at when you were 25 years old.

There is an increase in skill in older people and this coupled with the training over the years accounts for the better performances of the more mature athlete especially in the long-distance events. For those who may not have participated in athletics when they were young or gave it up for a period, coming back can be hard. The main barrier to cross is the psychological one that tells you to start at the same level as when you left off or at a level which you think you should be at when physically you are not at that stage. If you start off slowly and prepare carefully you will reach those higher levels you aspire to. Don't give up, keep plugging away, the opportunities are there for you. Although there is a decline in performance as you become older, training does enable you to fight the decline so that those who are running and taking exercise regularly will be much fitter than others of their age and in many cases fitter than people younger than themselves. Exercise can certainly help you stay younger.

For those coming into veterans' athletics, their aims need to be carefully considered. If an athlete formerly ran 800 metres, 1500 metres or one of the sprints then it would be unwise for him or her to come back into athletics as a veteran hoping to beat their personal bests. They could move up in distances, as Joyce has done, and then aim to achieve personal best performances. Alternatively they can aim for the standards of the veteran age group in which they would be competing. For instance the Road Runners Club of Great Britain operates a standards scheme whereby certificates are obtainable for times achieved over vetted courses. For 1982 the standards were:

| | 10 miles | 15 miles | 20 miles | Marathon |
|---|---|---|---|---|
| 1ST CLASS MEN | 0:53 | 1:23 | 1:54 | 2:35 |
| 2ND CLASS MEN | 1:01 | 1:37 | 2:16 | 3:05 |
| OVER 40 MEN | 1:03 | 1:40 | 2:20 | 3:10 |
| OVER 50 MEN | 1:10 | 1:50 | 2:30 | 3:25 |
| OVER 60 MEN | 1:17 | 2:00 | 2:45 | 3:45 |
| 1ST CLASS WOMEN | 1:00 | 1:33 | 2:08 | 2:54 |
| 2ND CLASS WOMEN | 1:08 | 1:48 | 2:30 | 3:27 |

Certificates are also available for other distances and although ladies' veteran certificates are not available in 1982, they will no doubt become available when the demand is there, just as over-60 age group standards for men were introduced in 1982.

Periodic check-ups with your doctor are always advisable just as regular dental inspections are necessary. Certainly those of you who haven't participated in any sport for some time and want to become involved in an active way would be best to have a chat with your doctor and let him or her know of your intentions.

Having received the all clear from your doctor to take up running you should immediately start those stretching exercises (see chapter 3) otherwise you could be back on your doctor's doorstep complaining of a sore Achilles' tendon or a pulled muscle. Remember, though, to do those exercises gently at first. Don't go pushing yourself too hard, if you cannot touch your toes, then aim to touch your ankles and progress from there.

If the veteran athlete has a disadvantage against the younger competitor he or she should be aiming to find some compensation for decline in some areas of performance. If you are a distance runner you might do this by improving style or at least paying careful attention to the way you run. Is the lower leg swinging through in a vertical line and not deviating away from the line along which you are running? Is as much drive as possible going through the centre of gravity of the body? Are the arms and shoulders providing a good counteraction to the leg drive?

*Often veterans will find themselves in the company of top runners. Kathryn Binns, a British international, passes a veteran during a 10-mile race.*

The veteran runner, like all athletes must remember that the more you want out the sport the more you have got to put in. Therefore to achieve good times, you need to put more into your training. But if your attitude is right, then there will be nothing to worry about and plenty to look forward to. The veteran runner is as old or as young as he or she feels and really perhaps veteran athletics may be the wrong name for those people who take part in athletics at the ripe old age of 35 for women and 40-plus for men. The word veteran has a ring of oldness to it. In America they don't have veteran championships, they have masters championships. The word master is a very suitable word to describe people who are continuing in a sport though it may have a certain sexist ring to it. I wonder what new words, what new developments, this exciting sport will offer next.

# APPENDIX (1)

**List of addresses of the running associations in English-speaking countries**

*Amateur Athletic Association* (responsible for men's athletics in England and Wales)
Francis House, Francis Street, London, SW1P 1DL.

*Women's Amateur Athletic Association* (responsible for women's athletics in England)
Francis House, Francis Street, London, SW1P 1DL.

*British Amateur Athletic Board* (responsible for international athletics in the United Kingdom)
Francis House, Francis Street, London, SW1P 1DL.

*Amateur Athletic Union of Australia* Grandstand, Olympic Park Athletic Track, Swan Street, Melbourne, 3002, Australia.

*Canadian Track and Field Association* 355 River Road, Tower "B", Vanier City, Ottawa, Ontario, KIL 8C1, Canada.

*New Zealand Amateur Athletic Association (Inc)* P.O. Box 741, Wellington, New Zealand.

*The Athletic Congress of the U.S.A. (Inc.)* P.O. Box 120, Indianapolis, Indiana, 46206, U.S.A.

# APPENDIX (2)

## Track running pace chart

| 200 | 300 | 400 | 600 | 800 | 1000 | 1200 | 1500 | 1 mile | 3000 | 5000 | 10,000 |
|---|---|---|---|---|---|---|---|---|---|---|---|
| 25·0 | 37·5 | 50 | 1:15·0 | 1:40·0 | | | | | | | |
| 26·0 | 39·0 | 52 | 1:18·0 | 1:44·0 | 2:10·0 | | | | | | |
| 27·0 | 40·5 | 54 | 1:21·0 | 1:48·0 | 2:15·0 | | | | | | |
| 28·0 | 42·0 | 56 | 1:24·0 | 1:52·0 | 2:20·0 | 2:48·0 | 3:30·0 | 3:45·3 | | | |
| 29·0 | 43·5 | 58 | 1:27·0 | 1:56·0 | 2:25·0 | 2:54·0 | 3:37·5 | 3:53·4 | | | |
| 30·0 | 45·0 | 60 | 1:30·0 | 2:00·0 | 2:30·0 | 3:00·0 | 3:45·0 | 4:01·4 | 7:30·0 | | |
| 31·0 | 46·5 | 62 | 1:33·0 | 2:04·0 | 2:35·0 | 3:06·0 | 3:52·5 | 4:09·5 | 7:45·0 | 12:55·0 | |
| 32·0 | 48·0 | 64 | 1:36·0 | 2:08·0 | 2:40·0 | 3:12·0 | 4:00·0 | 4:17·5 | 8:00·0 | 13:20·0 | 26:40·0 |
| 33·0 | 49·5 | 66 | 1:39·0 | 2:12·0 | 2:45·0 | 3:18·0 | 4:07·5 | 4:25·5 | 8:15·0 | 13:45·0 | 27:30·0 |
| 34·0 | 51·0 | 68 | 1:42·0 | 2:16·0 | 2:50·0 | 3:24·0 | 4:15·0 | 4:33·6 | 8:30·0 | 14:10·0 | 28:20·0 |
| 35·0 | 52·5 | 70 | 1:45·0 | 2:20·0 | 2:55·0 | 3:30·0 | 4:22·5 | 4:41·7 | 8:45·0 | 14:35·0 | 29:10·0 |
| 36·0 | 54·0 | 72 | 1:48·0 | 2:24·0 | 3:00·0 | 3:36·0 | 4:30·0 | 4:49·7 | 9:00·0 | 15:00·0 | 30:00·0 |
| 37·0 | 55·5 | 74 | 1:51·0 | 2:28·0 | 3:05·0 | 3:42·0 | 4:37·5 | 4:57·8 | 9:15·0 | 15:25·0 | 30:50·0 |
| 38·0 | 57·0 | 76 | 1:54·0 | 2:32·0 | 3:10·0 | 3:48·0 | 4:45·0 | 5:05·8 | 9:30·0 | 15:50·0 | 31:40·0 |
| 39·0 | 58·5 | 78 | 1:57·0 | 2:36·0 | 3:15·0 | 3:54·0 | 4:52·5 | 5:13·9 | 9:45·0 | 16:15·0 | 32:30·0 |
| 40·0 | 60·0 | 80 | 2:00·0 | 2:40·0 | 3:20·0 | 4:00·0 | 5:00·0 | 5:21·9 | 10:00·0 | 16:40·0 | 33:20·0 |
| 41·0 | 61·5 | 82 | 2:03·0 | 2:44·0 | 3:25·0 | 4:06·0 | 5:07·5 | 5:30·0 | 10:15·0 | 17:05·0 | 34:10·0 |
| 42·0 | 63·0 | 84 | 2:06·0 | 2:48·0 | 3:30·0 | 4:12·0 | 5:15·0 | 5:38·0 | 10:30·0 | 17:30·0 | 35:00·0 |
| 43·0 | 64·5 | 86 | 2:09·0 | 2:52·0 | 3:35·0 | 4:18·0 | 5:22·5 | 5:46·0 | 10:45·0 | 17:55·0 | 35:50·0 |
| 44·0 | 66·0 | 88 | 2:12·0 | 2:56·0 | 3:40·0 | 4:24·0 | 5:30·0 | 5:54·1 | 11:00·0 | 18:20·0 | 36:40·0 |
| 45·0 | 67·5 | 90 | 2:15·0 | 3:00·0 | 3:45·0 | 4:30·0 | 5:37·5 | 6:02·1 | 11:15·0 | 18:45·0 | 37:30·0 |
| 46·0 | 69·0 | 92 | 2:18·0 | 3:04·0 | 3:50·0 | 4:36·0 | 5:45·0 | 6:10·2 | 11:30·0 | 19:10·0 | 38:20·0 |
| 47·0 | 70·5 | 94 | 2:21·0 | 3:08·0 | 3:55·0 | 4:42·0 | 5:52·5 | 6:18·2 | 11:45·0 | 19:35·0 | 39:10·0 |
| 48·0 | 72·0 | 96 | 2:24·0 | 3:12·0 | 4:00·0 | 4:48·0 | 6:00·0 | 6:26·3 | 12:00·0 | 20:00·0 | 40:00·0 |

The chart indicates the speed of running required to attain specific times at even pace. For example to run a 1500 metres in 4 minutes 45 seconds, at level pace the 800 metres would be run in 2 minutes 32 seconds and the 400 metres in 76 seconds.

# WORLD DISTANCE RECORDS AS AT 31.8.1982

## Men

| | | |
|---|---|---|
| 800 metres | 1min. 41·73secs | Sebastian Coe (GB & NI) |
| 1500 metres | 3min. 31·36secs | Steve Ovett (GB & NI) |
| 1 mile | 3min. 47·33secs | Sebastian Coe (GB & NI) |
| 3000 metres | 7min. 32·01secs | Henry Rono (Kenya) |
| 5000 metres | 13min. 00·42secs | Dave Moorcroft (GB & NI) |
| 10000 metres | 27min. 22·5 secs | Henry Rono (Kenya) |
| Marathon | 2hrs. 08min. 13secs | Alberto Salazar (USA) |

## WOMEN

| | | |
|---|---|---|
| 800 metres | 1min. 53·43secs | Nadezhda Olizarenko (USSR) |
| 1500 metres | 3min. 53·47secs | Tatyana Kazankina (USSR) |
| 1 mile | 4min. 18·08secs | Mary Decker-Tabb (USA) |
| 3000 metres | 8min. 26·78secs | Svetlana Ulmasova (USSR) |
| 5000 metres | 15min. 08·26secs | Mary Decker-Tabb (USA) |
| 10000 metres | 31min. 35·3 secs | Mary Decker-Tabb (USA) |
| Marathon | 2hrs. 25min. 29secs | Allison Roe (NZ) |

You can appreciate the standard of the world records when you look at the pace required to set new world records on the track running pace chart. For instance to break the men's world 3000-metres record an athlete has almost to run the equivalent of 2 × 4-minute miles without any rest. If you try combining the marathon pace chart and the track pace chart it can be seen that Alberto Salazar's world marathon record is at 73 seconds/400-metres pace for the 26 miles 385 yards. Allison Roe was running at just over 82 seconds/400-metres pace in her world marathon best performance.

# APPENDIX (3)

## Marathon running pace chart

| 1 km | 1 mile | 5 km | 5 miles | 10 km | 15 km | 10 miles | 20 km | 15 miles | 25 km | 30 km | 20 miles | 35 km | 40 km | 25 miles | Marathon |
|---|---|---|---|---|---|---|---|---|---|---|---|---|---|---|---|
| 3:02·0 | 4:52·9 | 15:10 | 24:25 | 30:20 | 45:30 | 48:49 | 1:00:40 | 1:13:14 | 1:15:50 | 1:31:00 | 1:37:38 | 1:46:10 | 2:01:20 | 2:02:03 | 2:08:00 |
| 3:12·0 | 5:08·9 | 16:00 | 25:45 | 32:00 | 48:00 | 51:30 | 1:04:00 | 1:17:14 | 1:20:00 | 1:35:59 | 1:42:59 | 1:51:59 | 2:07:59 | 2:08:44 | 2:15:00 |
| 3:19·1 | 5:20·4 | 16:36 | 26:42 | 33:11 | 49:47 | 53:24 | 1:06:22 | 1:20:06 | 1:22:57 | 1:39:33 | 1:46:48 | 1:56:08 | 2:12:43 | 2:13:30 | 2:20:00 |
| 3:26·2 | 5:31·8 | 17:11 | 27:39 | 34:22 | 51:33 | 55:18 | 1:08:44 | 1:22:57 | 1:25:55 | 1:43:06 | 1:50:37 | 2:00:17 | 2:17:28 | 2:18:16 | 2:25:00 |
| 3:33·3 | 5:43·3 | 17:47 | 28:37 | 35:33 | 53:20 | 57:13 | 1:11:06 | 1:25:49 | 1:28:53 | 1:46:39 | 1:54:26 | 2:04:26 | 2:22:12 | 2:23:02 | 2:30:00 |
| 3:54·7 | 6:17·6 | 19:34 | 31:28 | 39:07 | 58:40 | 1:02:56 | 1:18:13 | 1:34:34 | 1:37:46 | 1:57:19 | 2:05:52 | 2:16:52 | 2:36:25 | 2:37:20 | 2:45:00 |
| 4:16·0 | 6:51·9 | 21:20 | 34:20 | 42:40 | 1:04:00 | 1:08:39 | 1:25:19 | 1:42:59 | 1:46:39 | 2:07:59 | 2:17:19 | 2:29:19 | 2:50:39 | 2:51:38 | 3:00:00 |
| 4:37·3 | 7:26·3 | 23:07 | 37:12 | 46:13 | 1:09:19 | 1:14:23 | 1:32:26 | 1:51:34 | 1:55:32 | 2:18:39 | 2:28:45 | 2:41:45 | 3:04:52 | 3:05:56 | 3:15:00 |
| 4:58·6 | 8:00·6 | 24:53 | 40:03 | 49:47 | 1:14:40 | 1:20:06 | 1:39:33 | 2:00:09 | 2:04:26 | 2:29:19 | 2:40:12 | 2:54:12 | 3:19:05 | 3:20:16 | 3:30:00 |
| 5:20·0 | 8:34·9 | 26:40 | 42:55 | 53:20 | 1:20:00 | 1:25:49 | 1:46:39 | 2:08:44 | 2:13:19 | 2:39:59 | 2:51:38 | 3:06:38 | 3:33:18 | 3:34:33 | 3:45:00 |
| 5:41·3 | 9:09·3 | 28:27 | 45:47 | 56:53 | 1:25:19 | 1:31:33 | 1:53:46 | 2:17:19 | 2:22:12 | 2:50:39 | 3:03:05 | 3:19:05 | 3:47:31 | 3:48:51 | 4:00:00 |
| 6:02·6 | 9:43·6 | 30:13 | 48:38 | 1:00:26 | 1:30:39 | 1:37:16 | 2:00:52 | 2:25:54 | 2:31:05 | 3:01:18 | 3:14:31 | 3:31:31 | 4:01:44 | 4:03:09 | 4:15:00 |
| 6:24·0 | 10:17·9 | 32:00 | 51:30 | 1:04:00 | 1:35:59 | 1:42:59 | 2:07:59 | 2:34:29 | 2:39:59 | 3:11:58 | 3:25:58 | 3:43:58 | 4:15:58 | 4:17:27 | 4:30:00 |
| 6:45·3 | 10:52·2 | 33:47 | 54:22 | 1:07:33 | 1:41:19 | 1:48:43 | 2:15:06 | 2:43:04 | 2:48:52 | 3:22:39 | 3:37:25 | 3:56:25 | 4:30:11 | 4:31:46 | 4:45:00 |
| 7:06·6 | 11:26·6 | 35:33 | 57:13 | 1:11:06 | 1:46:39 | 1:54:26 | 2:22:12 | 2:51:38 | 2:57:45 | 3:33:18 | 3:48:51 | 4:08:51 | 4:44:24 | 4:46:04 | 5:00:00 |

The marathon pace chart gives intermediate times for level pace running. For example, in a 3-hour marathon the 15-kilometre point would be passed in 1 hour, 4 minutes and the 20-miles point in 2 hours, 17 minutes, 19 seconds if level pace running was maintained. The world record by Alberto Salazar of 2 hours, 8 minutes and 13 seconds means running consecutive kilometres at 3:02·3 or consecutive miles at 4:53·4, while Allison Roe's world record of 2 hours, 25 minutes and 29 seconds represents 3:26·9 per kilometre or 5:32·9 per mile.

# Further reading

Our aim has been to encourage you to become a runner, or if you have started, to help you up the ladder of self-improvement. If, as we hope, you are now hooked on running, the publications listed below will help you learn more about the sport of athletics.

## MAGAZINES

*Athletics Weekly* 344 High Street, Rochester, Kent ME1 1DT.
*Marathon and Distance Runner* Peterson House, Northbank, Berryhill Industrial Est. Droitwich, Worcs. WR9 9BL.
*Running* 57–61 Mortimer Street, London W.1.
*Running* P.O. Box 10990, 1508 Oak St. Eugene, Oregon, 97440, U.S.A.
*Runner's World* 1400 Stierlin Road, Mountain View, CA. 94043, U.S.A.
*The Runner* P.O. Box 2730, Boulder, Colorado 80332, U.S.A.

## BOOKS

COSTILL, Dr. David L., *A Scientific Approach to Distance Running* (Track & Field News)
DICK, Frank, *Training Theory* (BAAB/AAA Publication)

149

LYDIARD, Arthur with GILMOUR, Garth, *Run the Lydiard Way* (Hodder & Stoughton)

TEMPLE, Cliff, *Cross Country and Road Running* (Stanley Paul & Co. Ltd.)

TEMPLE, Cliff, *Challenge of the Marathon*, A Runner's Guide (Stanley Paul & Co. Ltd.)

WATTS, Denis and WILSON, Harry, *Middle and Long Distance, Marathon and Steeplechase* (BAAB/AAA Publication)

WATTS, Denis, WILSON, Harry and HORWILL, Frank, *The Complete Middle Distance Runner* (Stanley Paul & Co. Ltd.)

WILSON, Neil, ETCHELLS, Andy with TULLOH, Bruce, *The Marathon Book.* (Virgin Books)

# Index

151